Praise for *The A-to-Z Social Workers and Ott*

CW00956402

Grise-Owens, Miller, & Eaves' *?*
Social Workers and Other Helpi
ed handbook to inspire and guide ~~self care practice.~~ Its insights
are far-ranging, original, practical, and flexible. The short chapter format, focused topics, and fresh tone are both accessible and sure to motivate. Even those who have given a great deal of thought and attention to self-care will find new, exciting, and practicable guidance in its pages.

Lisa D. Butler, Ph.D., Associate Professor
University at Buffalo, School of Social Work
Primary Developer, UBSSW *Self-Care Starter Kit*

The A-to-Z Self-Care Handbook for Social Workers and Other Helping Professionals is a wonderful addition to the field. It offers a broad range of concrete suggestions for improving individual self-care that should provide guidance and support to fit a broad range of practitioner needs. The book also includes material in several chapters noting the important role organizations must take in stress and burnout reduction and support of self-care. This combined focus on micro and macro approaches is necessary to move both individuals and the field forward in addressing stress and burnout.

Sue Steiner, Ph.D., MSW, Professor
School of Social Work at California State University, Chico
Co-author, *Self-Care in Social Work: A Guide for
Practitioners, Supervisors, and Administrators*

The A-to-Z Self-Care Handbook is a caring and useful resource for helping professionals concerned about burnout, stress, staff turnover, and wellness. It is presented in an accessible and easy-to-read format. It contains strategies, resources, and literally dozens of pointers for engaging in self-care. The central message is that we all have choices. By focusing on insights and reflections and providing resources and strategies, *The A-to-Z Self-Care Handbook* is a practical guide and an empowering book.

Dr. Barbara W. Shank, Ph.D., MSW, Dean and Professor,
School of Social Work, University of St. Thomas,
St. Catherine University
Chair, Board of Directors, Council on Social Work Education

Concentrated research on burnout and self-care that led to my latest book revealed that while the *Care* in Self-Care received a great deal of attention, the *Self* had almost been totally ignored. Only in recognizing and addressing this oversight can one select, integrate, and maintain individualized, personally appealing care strategies into day-to-day living, forever. Sometimes there is a book that speaks to what you also have tried to put into words that feels truly hand-in-glove. I see *The A-to-Z Self-Care Handbook for Social Workers and Other Helping Professionals* as precisely this book.

SaraKay Smullens, MSW, LCSW, author of *Burnout and Self-Care in Social Work: A Guidebook for Students and Those in Mental Health and Related Professions*

This book is an incredible gift to the dedicated professionals who have made it their life's work to help create healthier, happier, and more vibrant communities. As a licensed clinical social worker myself, I am thrilled that my colleagues and I now have a tool that we can share to help us continue to do the work we were called to do without sacrificing our own well-being. Its scholarly, research-based approach will make even the most academic-minded among us sit up and take notice of the importance of self-care, and yet it is structured in a way that makes it easy for busy professionals to apply these practices in their professional and personal lives. The authors took special care to ensure the guide could be customized, so that each of us can find what self-care really means to us. This comprehensive yet easy-to-navigate road map will allow all of us to achieve the balance needed to be in this important work for the long haul. As the leader of a large nonprofit organization, the health and well-being of my colleagues is always top of mind for me. This tool is just what an organization like ours needed to promote self-care in a way that makes sense for all of us!

Jennifer Hancock, LCSW, President & CEO
Volunteers of America—Mid-States

The A-to-Z
SELF-CARE
Handbook
for
Social Workers
and Other
Helping
Professionals

Edited by
Erlene Grise-Owens, Ed.D., LCSW, LMFT, MRE
Justin "Jay" Miller, Ph.D., CSW
Mindy Eaves, CSW, MSW

PRESS
Harrisburg, Pennsylvania

Published by:

PRESS

Post Office Box 5390
Harrisburg, PA 17110-0390 U.S.A.
717-238-3787 (voice)
717-238-2090 (fax)
http://www.socialworker.com

The New Social Worker Press is an imprint of White Hat Communications.

Quotes from Marianne Williamson's *A Return to Love* on pages 47-50 reprinted with permission.

Cover photo credit: Photo from BigStockPhoto.com © og-vision

Library of Congress Cataloging-in-Publication Data

Names: Grise-Owens, Erlene, editor.
Title: The A-to-Z self-care handbook for social workers and other helping professionals / edited by Erlene Grise-Owens, Ed.D., LCSW, LMFT, MRE, Justin "Jay" Miller, Ph.D., CSW, Mindy Eaves, CSW, MSW.
Description: Harrisburg, Pennsylvania : New Social Worker Press, 2016. | Description based on print version record and CIP data provided by publisher; resource not viewed.
Identifiers: LCCN 2016019851 (print) | LCCN 2016012171 (ebook) | ISBN 9781929109548 (E-book) | ISBN 9781929109531 (pbk.)
Subjects: LCSH: Social service–Handbooks, manuals, etc. | Self-consciousness
(Awareness)
Classification: LCC HV40 (print) | LCC HV40 .A798 2016 (ebook) | DDC 613.02/4361–dc23
LC record available at https://lccn.loc.gov/2016019851

Contents

Acknowledgments

Every worthwhile project takes a team— a body of people doing their part! We want to thank the A-to-Z team. First, we wish to express gratitude for each other, as friends, colleagues, and co-editors. Imagining this book together has required trust, humor, and the synergy of "sharing a brain." Also, we want to thank our core supporters, family, and friends. (You know who you are!) YOU are the best and most treasured part of our self-care plans!

Alongside us, as editors, we want to thank Linda Grobman for "getting" our brain-child/book proposal from the beginning and being such a wonderful partner. Your quiet enthusiasm, nitty-gritty attention to detail, dependable responses, and polite prompts have made the work a productive pleasure.

We could never have imagined this book without the many students and colleagues who inspired the book through shared journeys with us. You are the heart of this book. We are grateful for the A-to-Z contributors who made the book come to "real life" through their willingness to share their stories of struggles, successes, and strategies in self-care. Your vulnerability, resilience, creativity, and courage are the flesh and bones of this project.

Finally, we wish to acknowledge with open spirit the readers who will use this book and share it with others. You, our colleagues in the helping professions, are the veins that will give this book the life needed to contribute to a web of wellness in our work and world. We are grateful.

Co-Editors,
Erlene, Jay, & Mindy

Foreword

Self-care. We are thinking about it and talking about it a LOT. And that's a good thing.

Self-care is more than a buzzword. It is a real, and serious, issue for social workers and all helping professionals. As the editor and publisher of *The New Social Worker* magazine, I can tell you that our readers want more and more articles about self-care. The readers who are attracted to these articles are either already experiencing burnout or they have heard about burnout (or work with others who are experiencing it) and want to prevent it.

After all, what do we do for a living? We help others to take better care of themselves. To do this well and without impairment, we have to take care of ourselves.

Erlene Grise-Owens, Jay Miller, and Mindy Eaves are self-care role models. They are teaching the next generation of social workers about self-care and they're making it a high priority. By doing so, they are instilling in social work students the idea that self-care is an essential practice skill, not an "extra," and that it is an important component of ethical practice. They recognize, too, that self-care is important not only for social workers, but for *all* helping professionals.

And now they, along with their students and former students, are sharing their teaching and what they have learned along the way with you through this *Handbook.* Erlene, Jay, and Mindy came to me with a vision. They wanted to create a compact volume that would give readers some practical ways to look at self-care—something that would inspire as well as instruct readers in how to take charge of their own self-care plans. I could see and feel the excitement and the genuineness in their desire to spread a message of self-care as an essential practice skill.

As the book developed, I was excited to "hear" how each of the contributors had put self-care into practice in unique ways, both in their personal and their professional lives. I became inspired to take action toward my own self-care by using a FitBit-type tracker and smartphone apps to track my exercise, sleep, and nutrition.

You, the lucky new owner of this *Handbook*, are on your way to a SMART and viable self-care plan that will uniquely fit you and work for you. The concept of this book is simple. For each letter of the alphabet, a contributor has outlined a self-care strategy, including questions for reflection/discussion and additional resources for further exploration. Just as the ABCs are essential building blocks for a young child's learning, you can use the ABCs to build your way to a happy, healthy, ethical life as a helping professional.

You can use *Appendix A* and *Appendix B* to map out your self-care strategy. As suggested in the *Kaizen* entry, you can start small. Even if you take one practical strategy from this book and begin to use it regularly, it will make a difference. You can add to your self-care plan at your own pace.

This *Handbook's* value is not only in its usefulness as a self-care guide for individuals. I envision it being used as a tool by organizations as they support their workers' wellness, as well. It can be used in training and supervision, reinforcing the idea that self-care is an essential part of ethical and competent practice.

Self-care doesn't just happen on its own. It happens when you consciously seek out the tools to build a plan for it. With this book as a guide, you will have the tools to set specific goals and ways to reach them realistically.

Self-care is a lifestyle, not an emergency response. So let's get started!

Linda May Grobman, MSW, ACSW, LSW
Publisher/Editor, The New Social Worker Magazine

Chapter 1
Introduction and Overview

This compact book provides a structured format and an alphabetized array of strategies, resources, and pointers for engaging in self-care, as a core part of ethical professional practice for social workers and other helping professionals. The tone of the book is intended as collegial conversation, while providing a substantive, pragmatic resource. The accessible format is meant for busy professionals who do not necessarily want an academic tome on burnout, but who recognize—experientially—the need to address these concerns.

The book begins with an easily adaptable format for structuring self-care, as well as attention to accountability as essential in sustaining self-care. Then, the book offers brief entries from A to Z on key aspects of self-care. Written by practitioners for practitioners, each entry has been tested by the authors.

The *Handbook* can be used by individual practitioners to structure and support self-care. Also, the book is an ideal resource for supervisors, trainers, administrators, and other personnel responsible for professional development of employees in the helping professions. Similarly, the *Handbook* is an accessible text for educators and students who recognize the need to teach and learn about self-care as part of professional preparation. The book is a relevant resource that addresses the significant concern of burnout, through proactive engagement in self-care and wellness.

Why this Book?

Stress! Burnout! Compassion Fatigue! Secondary/Vicarious Trauma! Staff Turnover! These "conditions of professional depletion" (Greville, 2015, p. 14) are increasingly prevalent in helping professions (e.g., Mathieu, 2012; Papia, 2014, Skovholt & Trotter-Mathison, 2011; Smullens, 2012; Smullens, 2015; Van Dernoot Lipsky, 2009). This book is not a treatise on these troubling phenomena; it provides complementary resources that can be used to expand general knowledge on these topics.

However, if you are working in the field, you understand these terms, because you have lived them and/or observed colleagues live them. You see and/or experience being overwhelmed, stressed, and exhausted—with resultant health concerns, personal issues, and even professional impairment. These aspects have become all too commonplace in helping professions. Too often, they are accepted as just part of the terrain of professional helping. But they are not.

This *Handbook* focuses on prevention and reduction of these phenomena through structured, accessible, and practitioner-tested self-care and wellness strategies. Although drawing on research-based evidence, this book uses practice-based evidence. That is, real-life practitioners write about their everyday evidence/experience in implementing self-care.

Impetus and Background

This *Handbook* evolved from our MSW program's emphasis on teaching self-care as a professional practice skill. We have been incorporating specific assignments related to self-care into the social work curriculum for several years, including requiring that each student develop a specific self-care plan (Grise-Owens, Miller, Escobar-Ratliff, & George, in press). Notably, faculty do not grade the quality of the students' self-care. Rather, faculty give ongoing assessment and feedback on the students' critical and growing attention to this crucial aspect of professional practice.

In an advanced practice course sequence, an ongoing discussion board assignment asks students to share their successes, struggles, and strategies related to their self-care. (Most universities now use discussion boards as a part of a learning platform for online class participation, similar to an email or mailing list discussion.) Students participating in these discussions come from varied backgrounds; some have been in the field for many years and others are just beginning. Most of the students work full time while carrying a full graduate load, including a field practicum. Repeatedly, students spontaneously express how the discussion board on successes, struggles, and strategies is helpful and meaningful. They relate this experience to sustaining their professional practice.

As students/practitioners avidly shared their successes and struggles, they built a repository of strategies and resources. As one participant noted, "This discussion board [became] a think tank on self-care." From this "think tank," and the ongoing experience of seeing the impact of emphasizing self-care in professional development, faculty and students decided to create a resource book for busy professionals. Each A-to-Z entry in this book was generated from students' discussion board input. As evidenced in the contributors' biographical sketches, each entry is written by a practitioner. Thus, these entries extend the "think tank" into the broader professional community.

Professional Context and Key Caveat Regarding Organizational Wellness

Self-care is an imperative for ethical professional practice. Like other practice skills, self-care requires specific attention and skill development. As noted, Spalding University's MSW program has been incorporating attention to self-care as a practice skill for almost a decade. Concomitantly, in the broader context, helping professions increasingly recognize the deleterious effects of compassion fatigue, burnout, and vicarious trauma. The professional literature and professional standards have begun to emphasize self-care as a key antidote to these troubling phenomena (e.g., Barsky, 2014; Wharton, 2008).

Notably, in 2008, the National Association of Social Workers (U.S.) Delegate Assembly approved a policy statement on "Professional Self-Care and Social Work." This policy statement asserted that self-care is "an essential underpinning to best practice in the profession of social work" (2008, p. 268). NASW reported, "...self-care has not been fully examined or addressed within the profession" (p. 268). Further, NASW emphasized that professional development of social workers must include attention to self-care as professional practice. Similarly, the International Federation of Social Workers (IFSW) Statement of Ethical Principles (approved in 2004), states that social workers have a "duty to take necessary steps to care for themselves professionally and personally in the workplace and society" (Article 5, Professional Conduct, #6).

This emphasis on the ethical imperative means that self-care is not an "extra." Individual professionals have a clear responsibility to practice self-care. This book serves as a resource to support ethical practice and professional wellness through self-care.

At the same time, we (the editors and contributors) are compelled to emphasize an important caveat. In offering a resource for practicing individual self-care, we do not downplay or deny the very real organizational dynamics and conditions that can create toxic, unhealthy, and unsupportable environments. Larger systems—including human service organizational cultures—must be acknowledged and addressed. One of the entries, *Organizational Wellness,* explicitly speaks to this important issue.

This resource can also be used by supervisors and administrators to promote a healthier organizational culture. Through using this *Handbook* for staff development, organizations can promote wellness. Likewise, through using this *Handbook* for curricula, educators can influence practitioners and organizational leaders who will learn—in their professional programs—how to promote wellness.

How to Use this Book

First and foremost, we hope you will use this *Handbook* in whatever manner is most helpful to you. The way you use this resource may vary, depending on your individual circumstances, professional context, and role. Here are some overarching suggestions.

The *Handbook* can be used as an individual tool for self-care as a professional practice skill. Each entry is written by a practitioner who implemented that particular aspect of self-care. Even if using the book primarily as an individual guide, we encourage using the self-care planning process and having accountability measures. (See Chapter 2.)

The *Handbook* can also be used in groups, such as staff development, supervision, and peer support. These groups can be as large as staff training efforts or as small as two or three people who commit to an accountability group. This resource can be used for ongoing staff meetings. Each entry can serve as a discussion topic for staff meetings (either face-to-face or virtual) that include an agenda item of self-care/staff wellness. Or, the *Handbook* can be adapted for structured staff training or continuing education offerings. The *Handbook* would be an ideal resource for an extended staff retreat—with perhaps ongoing follow-up for ongoing implementation. Similarly, the *Handbook* can be used to guide individual supervision or small group supervision.

Likewise, this resource can be used in social work and other professional preparation curricula. As noted, this book evolved from a discussion board experience of MSW students in an Advanced Social Work Practice course sequence. Similarly, other programs could use this *Handbook* as a text. This resource can be used by field supervisors, faculty, and/or program directors to incorporate self-care as professional practice into the curriculum. Developing this skill as early as possible in professional training is essential for long-term effectiveness and well-being of practitioners.

Each entry has questions at the end to guide personal reflection, with the intent of deepening attention to this element of self-care. These questions can be used to guide individual reflection. Additionally, the questions can provide discussion points for the group.

We suggest using this overarching question as you consider each entry: *What are your successes, struggles, and strategies related to this topic?* As with any growth/change endeavor, self-care efforts need to build on successes. So, in reflection, you may remember times when you were more successful in a particular area of self-care. For instance, you may recall that you had better success with exercise when you exercised in the morning before going to work. In your updated self-care plan, you can consider how to recapture that success. Similarly, as social beings, we find it helpful and hopeful to share our struggles. Hearing about how others have struggled with self-care—in various areas—can reinforce that "we are all in this together." Likely, you will learn many helpful strategies—both through the A-to-Z entries and through discussion with colleagues.

In a workplace environment, these strategies can be incorporated to affect the work culture. For instance, a strategy may be to carve out time for a lunch break, away from your desk. Others in the organization can reinforce this strategy by agreeing to remind each other of this important self-care commitment. Supervisors can reinforce this strategy by incorporating staggered lunch times or other supports.

Also, each entry includes sample resources that the writer found particularly helpful or pivotal in understanding the topic. These resources are merely examples of varied resources available. They serve to encourage the reader to explore what may be most accessible and meaningful for you. Also, we include selected resources on broader topics related to self-care. These resources, although not comprehensive, provide materials that can augment any self-care endeavor. For instance, a staff trainer may want to provide an overview presentation of the phenomena of burnout, vicarious trauma, and compassion fatigue in introducing a self-care initiative in the organization. These additional resources will provide ready references to get you started and augment ongoing self-care efforts.

While organized in an A-to-Z format, it is not necessary to follow the book in a linear fashion. For instance, you may flip to an entry that you find most challenging, as a starting point. For example, if you identify sleep as a key concern in your self-care, you may want to begin with Carmen's *Zzzz—Sleep* entry. Or, if you are unsure about the need for self-care, you may begin with Eileen's *A—Awareness* entry. Similarly, depending on the structure and allotted timeframe—i.e., individual reflection, supervision meetings, coursework, staff training, and so forth—you may want to focus on one entry for discussion at each meeting, take larger segments, or even the entire book in one training.

Just as the letters of the alphabet can be used to form myriad words and sentences, we hope that you will use the A-to-Z basics of this *Handbook* to design your own meaningful structure for self-care. We sincerely hope you will keep this book handy for many years to come and that you will share it with others. If you are in a supervisory or administrative role, we hope you will use the *Handbook* as an impetus to promote organizational wellness through attention to staff self-care. Together, let's reinforce a web of wellness through A-to-Z attention to self-care as an essential professional practice skill.

Selected Resources

Barsky, A. (2014). Being conscientious: Ethics of impairment and self care. *The New Social Worker, 22*(1), 4-5.

Greville, L. (2015). Self-care solutions: Facing the challenge of asking for help. *Social Work Today, 15*(3), 14-15.

Grise-Owens, E., Miller, J., Escobar-Ratliff, L., & George, N. (in press). Teaching self-care/wellness as a professional practice skill: A curricular case example. *Journal of Social Work Education.*

International Federation of Social Workers. (2004). *Statement of ethical principles.* Retrieved from *http://ifsw.org/policies/statement-of-ethical-principles/*

Mathieu, F. (2012). *The compassion fatigue workbook: Creative tools for transforming compassion fatigue and vicarious traumatization.* New York: NY: Routledge.

National Association of Social Workers. (2008). Professional self-care and social work. In NASW, *Social work speaks: NASW policy statement 2009-2012* (pp. 268-272). Washington, DC: Author.

Papia, D. M. (2014). Burnout and self-care: A process of helping, *The New Social Worker, 21(4).* Retrieved from *http://www.socialworker.com/feature-articles/practice/burnout-and-self-care-a-process-in-helping/*

Skovholt, T. M., & Trotter-Mathison, M. (2011). *The resilient practitioner—Burnout prevention and self-care strategies for counselors, therapists, teachers, and health professionals.* New York, NY: Routledge.

Smullens, S. (2012). What I wish I had known: Burnout and self-care in our social work profession. *The New Social Worker, 19*(4), 6-9.

Smullens, S. (2015). *Burnout and self-care in social work: A guidebook for students and those in mental health and related professions.* Washington, DC: NASW Press.

Van Dernoot Lipsky, L. (with Burk, C.). (2009). *Trauma stewardship: An everyday guide to caring for self while caring for others.* San Francisco, CA: Berrett-Koehler.

Wharton, T. C. (2008). Compassion fatigue: Being an ethical social worker. *The New Social Worker, 15*(1), 4-7.

Chapter 2

Using a Self-Care Plan and Accountability to Structure Use of the A-to-Z Strategies

Unfortunately, self-care does not just happen. It requires intentionality, structure, and accountability. Jackson (2014) contends that self-care is a "core competency" for professional social workers. As such, it requires intentional attention. Our MSW program has developed self-care as a professional practice skill in the curriculum, with focused assignments. Faculty have also offered "well-shops" for the professional community (i.e., continuing education offerings and staff trainings) on self-care as an essential practice skill.

We have found that *using a specific, structured self-care plan form is essential for ensuring intentional attention to self-care.* We provide the easily adaptable *Self-Care Plan Form* (Appendix A). We also provide a completed self-care plan as an example (Appendix B). Use this form to list goals in categories of physical, emotional, social, and professional—with spiritual care included in any of these categories.

Notably, this self-care plan incorporates both personal and professional self-care. Lee and Miller (2013) provide a useful discussion on the reciprocal relationship between personal self-care and professional self-care. The A-to-Z entries in this *Handbook* give attention to both arenas. That is, entries such as "Supervision" pertain to professional self-care, and entries such as "Exercise" pertain to personal self-care.

A self-care assessment may be helpful in thinking through areas for attention. Lisa D. Butler (n.d.), associate professor at the University at Buffalo School of Social Work, created a starter kit for self-care, which includes a self-care assessment form. Also, Cox and Steiner's book (2013) and companion website (n.d.) include resources, such as a workplace stress scale and "Sources of Stress" worksheet. These complementary resources can inform your self-care plan and augment your A-to-Z development.

As with any planned change, self-care goals need to be attainable and measurable. We use the popular acronym: SMART, i.e., Specific, Measurable, Achievable, Realistic, and Time-limited. (The SMART strategy is commonly attributed to Peter Drucker [1954], the well-known business leader and author.) Too often, people become discouraged in their self-care efforts because they do not use best practices in their own self-care practice!

Please note that the planning form is an organic document. We encourage you to establish an initial self-care plan, before beginning the A-to-Z process delineated in this book. Then, as you use this *Handbook,* the A-to-Z entries will help you refine and strengthen your self-care plan. As you become more informed and engaged with your self-care, you can adapt and refine your plan. Likewise, as your circumstances change, you may need to adjust your self-care plan to be SMART in a way that supports success. Remember that YOU define success. (See *K—Kaizen Method: Small Changes=Significant Effects* entry.)

For example, on her self-care plan "Shanda, the Social Worker" set a physical goal to "eat better." This goal was not SMART; Shanda felt like a failure and became discouraged in her self-care efforts. Through the A-to-Z discussion, Shanda adjusted her goal to eat less than 1500 calories daily, except for Sundays. She based this goal on tracking her food intake for several days. She also did a Google search to get information about what her calorie intake needed to be if she wanted to lose weight gradually. Shanda recognized that her family had high-calorie Sunday dinners, which were too hard for her to resist. (Besides, this family time was part of her psychological self-care plan: *B—Balance.*) Shanda's revised physical goal is specific, measureable, achievable, realistic, and time-limited. With this SMART goal, Shanda was able to improve her self-care. Likewise, in the A-to-Z discussion, Shanda learned about other simple strategies for healthy diet, such as the effect of water on health. She began tracking (and increasing) her water intake, along with her calorie count. (See *D—Diet* entry.)

In addition to SMART planning, we emphasize that accountability is key in self-care efforts. The last column in the self-care planning form relates to accountability measures. This column requires specificity about how you will know if you are implementing the self-care strategy. Continuing the example above, Shanda used a "Calorie Tracking" app to track her calorie intake. Other typical accountability measures include journaling; calendar appointments; charts; and other tracking forms, apps, or tools.

We also encourage *using accountability partners or groups* to sustain self-care efforts. In our MSW program, students form two- to three-member accountability groups. These groups serve to support, challenge, and encourage each other to stay on track with self-care efforts. (See *C— Connection* entry.)

So, now, let's get started with self-care. Self-care as a practice skill is as essential and basic as learning your ABCs. With these fundamental elements, your self-care will be SMART and your professional practice will be more meaningful, enjoyable, and effective.

Selected Resources

Butler, L. D. (n.d.). *Self-care starter kit.* Retrieved from *http://socialwork.buffalo.edu/resources/self-care-starter-kit/ developing-your-self-care-plan.html*

Cox, K., & Steiner, S. (2013). *Self-care in social work: A guide for practitioners, supervisors, and administrators.* Washington, DC: NASW Press.

Cox, K., & Steiner, S. (n.d.). Self-care in social work. Retrieved from *http://www.selfcareinsocialwork.com/about/*

Drucker, P. (1954). *The practice of management.* New York, NY: Harper & Row.

Jackson, K. (2014). Social worker self-care—The overlooked core competency, *Social Work Today, 14, 3-14.*

Lee, J. J., & Miller, S. E. (2013). A self-care framework for social workers: Building a strong foundation for practice. *Families in Society: The Journal of Contemporary Social Services, 94(2), 96-103.*

Chapter 3
The A-to-Z Entries

Awareness
Eileen Krueger

Change cannot occur without first becoming aware. The first step in any growth process or skill development is awareness. So, awareness is a foundational—and ongoing—part of self-care practice.

Self-Care and the Change Process

Self-care was infused (enthusiastically!) into the MSW program where I was a student, at Spalding University. This emphasis included reading Clemans' (2008) brief article on vicarious traumatization. Clemans identified awareness, balance, and connection as ways to attend to self-care. As a survivor of breast cancer, I have a particular awareness of the value of my health. But, before my MSW experience, I had no awareness of how self-care was linked to avoiding stress and professional burnout. At first, in learning about self-care, I experienced ambivalence. I thought it sounded like a good idea, but, honestly, it felt like one more thing to add to my already full plate! I wasn't sure if I was ready for this self-care commitment.

The process I went through in my engagement with self-care is similar to the change cycle delineated in the Motivational Interviewing (MI) approach. MI deals explicitly with the ambivalence and resistance that is natural in any change effort (e.g., Miller & Rollnick, 2012). Awareness, leading to change and implementing self-care, involved these MI phases:

- acknowledgment that I might not be taking such great care of myself *(pre-contemplation);*
- recognition that I should be taking better care of myself, along with the sensibility that I had the ability to make changes in this area, which included a self-care plan *(preparation);*
- experimentation with self-care and figuring out what works *(action and maintenance);* and
- adaptation: I must realize that self-care is not a "done deal" *(relapse).* I know that I have to adapt and re-commit at times (back to *pre-contemplation*).

Self-Compassion, Self-Talk, and Self-Care

A key shift in moving out of my "ambivalence" and part of my awareness-building was acknowledging that I was important enough to merit self-care. This awareness relates to self-compassion and self-talk. One of my colleagues made an insightful observation about self-compassion, self-care, and self-talk. She noted that she would not talk to/relate to anybody else the way she treated herself—putting herself down or just ignoring her own needs. As a mother of three, I am used to thinking of and caring for others. Putting the focus on myself first is a challenge.

So, what is self-compassion? Kristin Neff (2015) writes and presents extensively on this topic. Her website has an array of helpful resources. Neff defines self-compassion as being empathic and understanding to oneself. She clarifies that self-compassion is not selfish nor is it self-pity, and it does not excuse accountability. But self-compassion, like compassion in general, is about being kind and considerate—toward oneself!

Learning To Be Kind and Considerate

I have learned that in order to be a healthy and effective helping professional, one must be kind and considerate of oneself. One must have an ongoing relationship with self-care. I encourage you to incorporate this awareness of self-care into your life with a SMART plan. Learn from my mistakes.

Your plan doesn't need to be filled with lofty goals. Instead, go for awareness in basic areas of struggle. Set realistic goals like getting adequate sleep, drinking enough water (and not just coffee) throughout the day, eating healthy foods, and getting exercise (such as seizing opportunities for a walk at lunch or taking the stairs instead of the elevator). New patterns will begin to emerge through your awareness.

Informed by paying attention to my daily and weekly schedule, my awareness led to some concrete plans for being kind and considerate to myself. For example, my SMART plan includes nutrition basics, including getting to the grocery store on a regular basis and planning in advance for practical and healthy meals. These plans/actions result in my having the time and the ingredients on hand to quickly prepare dinner. Thus, dinnertime has become less chaotic and more predictable (not to mention providing us with leftovers to take for lunch the next day). This change is much SMARTer than ordering a pizza and eating it with my daughter as we stand at the kitchen counter! This change has also had a ripple effect in other areas of my life.

I think part of the awareness needs to include an element of spirituality as important to one's well-being. Spirituality is about creating meaning. This element can mean anything from attending church, temple, or mosque; to practicing mindfulness techniques, such as meditation or Yoga; to simply connecting with nature. Awareness in this area is key to a well-balanced self-care plan. Two books have helped me with the awareness of being mindful. The books were given to me, at two very different stages of my life, by my dear friend (a spiritual guru). The first one is *Everyday Sacred: A Woman's Journey Home* by Sue Bender. The second book is *Simple Abundance: A Daybook of Comfort and Joy* by Sarah Ban Breathnach. Both books have helped me become aware. They help me appreciate simple wisdom, in finding the importance in small things and in finding life's comfort and joy every single day. This meaning-making helps me be more compassionate.

You don't have to develop a perfect plan today—or even an imperfect one. Start with becoming aware. Go forth and let some new insights emerge. Get started by using the SMART plan to create some lifestyle changes to reinforce wellness, as an essential professional practice skill.

Reflection/Discussion

1. Where are you in the change process related to self-care? What ambivalence do you feel?
2. Consider the connection between self-compassion, self-talk, and self-care. Take Neff's brief self-compassion scale (*http://self-compassion.org/test-how-self-compassionate-you-are/*). Consider what your score means.
3. We hope the entries in this *Handbook* will help you become more aware, more prepared, and more able to pursue YOUR self-care. What are YOUR next steps toward becoming more aware of self-care?

Selected Resources

Bender, S. (1996). *Everyday sacred: A woman's journey home.* New York, NY: HarperCollins.

Breathnach, S. B. (1995). *Simple abundance: A daybook of comfort and joy.* New York, NY: Warner Books.

Clemans, S. E. (2008). Understanding vicarious traumatization—Strategies for social workers. *Social Work Today, 4*(2), 13-17.

Miller W. R., & Rollnick, S. (2012). *Motivational interviewing: Helping people change* (3rd ed.). New York, NY: Guilford Press.

Neff, K. (2015). *Self-compassion: The proven power of being kind to yourself.* New York, NY: HarperCollins.

Balance: Deciding to Live on Purpose and With Purpose

Denisa Hobbs

In this hurried existence we call life, creating balance can seem elusive. Clemans (2008) listed "balance" as the second of three basics of self-care. I have read lots of advice on balancing work, home, and school life. Many well intended authors seem to suggest that people looking for balance learn to "juggle it all, just better." Although this may be status quo for many, I propose, in finding balance with self-care, we learn to: Decide! Decide what is important, and work at that.

Balance: Challenging the Illusion

Unfortunately, I learned this lesson in a "trial by fire." During my junior year of college, my husband passed away. It was life altering. My confidante, my co-parenting partner of four children, my help, and the many other things he represented was gone. I didn't have much aid in the way of family and friends. As such, my life took a turn that I had never experienced. As a student, an only parent, an employee, and a new home owner, I wanted to juggle it all. I thought I needed to juggle it all; if I didn't do it, who would?

However, after a few months, I became the Jack/Jill of all trades and the master of none. It broke me mentally, emotionally, spiritually, and physically. At this stage, I knew I needed *true* balance in my life. That's when I learned that *deciding* was my greatest self-care tool.

Fuentes, Ogden, Ryan-Haddad, and Strang (2015) challenged the view of balance as an illusion. They advised to make deliberate choices and look at the idea of life balance as a myth. Sitting with the notion that life balance, as I understood it, was a myth took a load off my shoulders. I had three school-aged children in three different schools, needing help with schoolwork, saxophone lessons, football or basketball practice, library club, and on and on. Still, I had to care for myself and make sure I made my own academic deadlines (not to mention dinner and housework). I found comfort in knowing that trying to maintain what most would consider life balance was as elusive as grasping oxygen out of thin air.

Instead, I learned to decide. I decided to deal with one child at a time. I decided to attend one parent-teacher conference in a given day. I decided to concentrate on one assignment at a time. And, as hard as it was for me to do in my situation, at certain times, I decided to ask for help. I made a lot of conscious decisions. And, as implausible as it sounds, it made my life much better. I still had responsibilities. But learning to make decisions provided me with a way to practice balance in all the things I had going on in my life.

Redefining Balance

Self-care is an intentional discipline, which requires balance. In finding balance, we must look introspectively at our lives, decide what is important enough to have our time and attention, and take action to do that well. Merriam-Webster (n.d.) defines balance as "a state in which different things occur in equal or proper amounts." To admit that we need balance is to admit that many things are important to us. However, we need to remind ourselves not to fall into the myth of "a life well balanced," but instead to view life as well decided.

Admittedly, many times we can keep balance by deciding to focus on situations and circumstances in allotted time frames, which relieves us from "dropping balls" when attempting to maintain all we do. Fuentes et al. (2015) listed five elements of focus to help keep life decisive and deliberate:

1. define personal success;
2. manage technology and connectedness;
3. build and maintain support networks;
4. collaborate with partners; and
5. choose selectively on opportunities in our professional and personal lives.

With these five areas of focus, we can live our day-to-day lives *on* purpose and *with* purpose.

Each person may define balance differently. An Indian proverb says that each person is like a house with four rooms: physical, emotional, spiritual, and mental. Most of us tend to live in one room most of the time. But we need to go into every room to be complete. One of my colleagues in my MSW cohort made a discovery about his balance, while completing the self-care form used in our program (see Appendix A). He shared that, as an introvert, he relished time alone. But he was neglecting the social aspect of his life. Upon reflection, he decided to be more intentional about scheduling time with friends and family. He even volunteered to take his young nephews and their family dog to the park for a weekly romp. He reported that this change in the social aspect of his life helped him feel more balanced in all areas.

There will always be appointments, deadlines, events, and even moments that can't be replicated. Each of us has unique dynamics in our lives. Maintaining balance requires that we decide where we will give our attention, time, affection, and effort. This deciding requires deliberation and resolve. Being an only parent, a child, a daughter, a student, a volunteer, a friend, and an employee takes a great deal of planning and deciding. But I have learned that when done with decisiveness, "balance" can be maintained.

Reflection/Discussion

1. What are your thoughts about balance being a myth?
2. What decisions do you need to make that would help you be better balanced?
3. Consider times you needed balance. How did you handle it?

Selected Resources

Balance [Def. 3]. (n.d.). In *Merriam Webster Online.* Retrieved July 15, 2015, from *http://www.merriam-webster.com/dictionary/balance*

Clemans, S.E. (2008). Understanding vicarious traumatization—Strategies for social workers. *Social Work Today, 4*(2), 13-17.

Fuentes, D. G., Ogden, R. R., Ryan-Haddad, A., & Strang, F. (2015). Reframing our pursuit of life balance. *American Journal of Pharmaceutical Education, 79*(3), 1-4.

Connection
Sean Hagan

The topic of "Connection" resonates with me because, in 2010, I began my journey of 12-Step recovery from alcoholism and addiction. I've since focused time, energy, and effort to connect with healthier people, places, and things. Through the recovery process, I've become better connected with myself. I've learned vital lessons about who I am and who I'm not.

In her brief article, Clemans (2008) listed "connection" as the final element of her "ABC" delineation of self-care pointers. She noted the importance of positive connections in supporting self-care. Earlier in this *Handbook,* the editors encouraged the intentional use of self-care accountability/ support partners or small groups; this connection is key in supporting self-care. The following entry elaborates on connection as a core element of self-care and highlights how the A-to-Z entries in this *Handbook* are connected.

Perhaps everything is connected in some way. Who, where, what, when, how, and why are we connected? Merriam-Webster's (2015) online dictionary has several helpful definitions for connection, including "political, social, professional, or commercial relationship"; "a set of persons associated together"; and "a relation of personal intimacy." We are connected with people, plants, animals, hobbies, interests, businesses, organizations, places, things, and more.

Connected with Whom, Where, and What?

People are connected with many other people. According to Yalom & Leszcz (2005), "People need people—for initial and continued survival, for socialization, for the pursuit of satisfaction" (p. 24). With ubiquitous social media, it's easier than ever to get connected and stay connected with people. More than 1.5 billion people worldwide are now on Facebook, which means we can easily connect with people around the world in myriad ways (Leading Social Networks,

2015). Common groups of people we may connect with include: family, friends, co-workers, customers, clients, associates, hobby and interest groups, clubs, religious and spiritual organizations, social service organizations, mentors, teachers, and students.

Similarly, most of us go places daily, such as to work, school, daycare, restaurants, grocery stores, parks, houses of family and friends, and vacation spots. Most people have hobbies and interests, which can connect us with other people, nature, objects, brands, services, and more. For example, hobbies can connect us with cars, music, sports, entertainment, and activities. How do people decide on products, services, and brands (Rani, 2014)? Some people research the brands and where they shop. Many consider cost and perceived value. How do we choose where we go and what we do? Do these places promote self-care or cause stress? Do we balance where we spend our time and energy? We can form identity and connection with ourselves by understanding our own values and pursuing these values through our buying habits and how we structure our activities. (See entries *Time* and *Values* for connected discussion.)

Connected When and How?

Today, with social media and other means, people have many ways to stay connected. In our fast paced world, it's important to ask ourselves, "When and how am I connected?" Is it healthy to be connected at all times? Could over-connection lead to being overwhelmed? Self-care is meant to help a person stay physically, emotionally, mentally, and spiritually healthy. So, are you connected at all times? How often do you check your phone for missed calls, text messages, tweets, emails, notifications, and the like? Do you ever allow yourself to disconnect from the stressors of the world, so you can reconnect with yourself? (See *Diet* entry.)

One way that I disconnect from everything else is to reconnect with myself through prayer and meditation. I connect through prayer to the God of my own understanding, who I think of as a Spirit of the Universe. That is, I believe in some Force in life greater than myself, who helps connect us all. I pray each morning and each night, as well as through-out the day, which helps to center my thoughts and actions. Of course, not everyone believes in a God or a Spirit of the Universe.

Each person's perspective is unique. Hopefully, every-one has some belief in him- or herself and perhaps the Heal-ing Power of Human-Kind. You may find that meditation helps you connect. Many people also enjoy yoga, tai chi, martial arts, or other activities that aim to focus, relax, and discipline the mind, while letting go and momentarily dis-connecting from the responsibilities and stressors of the world.

I've learned that I can maintain better connection by practicing spiritual principles, such as honesty, patience, faith, love, tolerance, understanding, gratitude, forgive-ness, and courage. When I'm practicing spiritual princi-ples, I feel better about myself and those people, places, and things around me. Practicing spiritual principles is something I can do in all of my affairs, including with fam-ily, friends, employment, service work, or any other situa-tion or person I encounter. On the other hand, when I have anger and fear in my life, especially self-centered fear, I am more likely to cause some level of harm to myself or oth-ers. Anger and fear disconnect me from myself. The more I rely on spiritual principles to cope with anger and fear rather than relying on defects of character, defense mech-anisms, or inappropriate behavior, the more connected I am with myself and others (Alcoholics Anonymous, 2001). (See entries—*Fear, Mindfulness, Nature,* and *eXpressive* arts for connected discussion.)

Why: Connecting it All Together

Connection is fundamental to human existence. We can't exist independently; we need each other. As Yalom and Leszcz (2005) stated, "The need to belong is a powerful, fundamental, and pervasive motivation" (p. 19). That is, our connections are integral to our well-being. All living things are connected. The most essential and basic connection is through our breath.

Human beings and animals take in oxygen and release carbon dioxide. Plants, in turn, take in carbon dioxide and release oxygen. This connection illustrates a simple yet powerful fact of nature: humans' breath physically connects them with all of the plants in the world, as well as with all human beings and animals. When we consider that we really are all connected and that we all make up this one world called Planet Earth, hopefully, we can move more toward true empathy, compassion, and love for one another.

In my own life journey, when I began to acknowledge how connected the whole world is, I became motivated to move away from being selfish, self-centered, and self-serving. Then I was able to grow toward being more selfless, others-centered, and serving of others. When I'm working toward the latter ideal, I am working toward spiritual progress. In a profound way, self-care helps maintain the connection that allows me to be less selfish and more others-serving.

Self-care is vital to the health and well-being of all human beings, especially to professionals who provide care for others. I invite you to consider and evaluate the connections present in your life and how they relate to your self-care. As you continue to use this *Handbook,* you will see how the different elements of a self-care plan are connected. Ongoing attention to this connection can help with sustaining meaningful and effective self-care. My hope is that each person, during his or her life journey, will choose to pursue better and healthier connections with self, others, and the Universe through the process of self-actualization and self-care.

Reflection/Discussion

1. How do you define "connection"? When do you feel connected in a holistic and healthy way? How could you be more intentional with each connection? For example, could your self-care plan include daily connection through prayer and meditation or a walk in nature?
2. Close your eyes for a few minutes and take some deep breaths. While meditating, contemplate on how your breath connects you with every entity in the world.

After this meditation, reflect on: "Do my thoughts and actions demonstrate that we are all connected?" (See *Gratitude* entry.)

3. Make a "self-care eco-map." Many social workers and other helping professionals are familiar with using eco-maps with our clients. An eco-map is a snapshot in time of a person's informal and formal support systems. Eco-maps are useful tools to help map out, visualize, and better understand connections. (For a refresher on creating an eco-map, search the Internet for "How to create an eco-map.")

List at least five people with whom you feel most connected. List the person's name and the common connection(s) between you and this person. Draw an arrow from your name to each person. Draw an arrow from each person also connected with each other. Consider your relationship with each person. For each relationship, make a list of the common behaviors and ways of acting that you rely on within the connection. Does your interaction with this person improve your self-care plan through relief of anxiety, stress, and the burdens of life? Or, does this person or interaction contribute negatively? Consider ways the connection with each person could improve your self-care. (See *Relationships* entry for connected discussion.)

Likewise, list all the places you go throughout a typical week, such as school, work, the homes of family and friends, businesses, restaurants, health spas, 12-Step meetings, spiritual places, and so forth. Beside each place, note the reason(s) you go to this place. Then, examine whether this place aids in or detracts from your self-care. How can you increase your connection with the places that support your wellness and limit the places that do not? Also, consider how you can adapt those environments where you spend a lot of time. (See *Workspace* entry for more discussion.)

4. Use the previous eco-map exercise to explore your personal values in life. How do you make decisions, structure your time, and allocate money and other resources? Are these congruent with your values? How could

you use your self-care plan to be more authentic and congruent? (See *Awareness* and *Balance* entries.)

Selected Resources

Alcoholics Anonymous. (2001). *Alcoholics Anonymous, 4th Edition.* New York, NY: A.A. World Services.

Leading social networks worldwide as of January 2016, ranked by number of active users (in millions). (2016). Retrieved from *http://www.statista.com/statistics/272014/global-social-networks-ranked-by-number-of-users/*

Clemans, S. E. (2008). Understanding vicarious traumatization—Strategies for social workers. *Social Work Today, 4*(2), 13-17.

Connection. (2015). In *Merriam-Webster online.* Retrieved from *http://www.merriam-webster.com/dictionary/connection*

Rani, P. (2014). Factors influencing consumer behavior. *Institute of Law Kurukshetra, University Kurukshetra, India, 2*(9), 52-61.

Work/life balance and stress management. (2013). In *Queensland Government online.* Retrieved from *https://www.qld.gov.au/health/mental-health/balance/lifestyle/index.html*

Yalom, I. D., & Leszcz, M. (2005). *The theory and practice of group psychotherapy.* New York, NY: Basic Books.

Diet: What Are You "Feeding" Yourself? Body, Mind, and Spirit

Amee Ramsey

Self-care is an organic, individualized, and holistic process—not a perfect, one-approach-fits-all endeavor. Our diet, what we are feeding ourselves, is a crucial step in the self-care process. In my journey toward discovering self-care, I have learned that my physical and emotional well-being is directly related to what I am "feeding" myself. I believe that, with all things in life, moderation and balance are key.

Body

Being a social worker or other helping professional is demanding on the body, mind, and spirit. I have found that developing a relationship with my body allows me to take care of it better. Two important ways I care for my body are: diet and exercise. Self-care is a personal process. I make food choices that may not work for others. The key is discovering what does and does not work for you. I choose a stricter diet, because I have found I do better with structure—even with food! I will treat myself, but I practice moderation even when I splurge. "You are what you eat" is a phrase we hear time and time again. I know that when I am eating healthy (lots of fruits and vegetables; less sugar and processed food), I feel healthier.

Healthy choices can be small. The Centers for Disease Control and Prevention (CDC) reports that "substituting water for one 20-ounce sugar sweetened soda will save you about 240 calories" (n.d., para. 6). Consuming an adequate amount of water is a simple step that can have a significant impact. Reducing calories is not the only benefit of drinking more water. The CDC reports that water regulates temperature, lubricates and cushions joints, and protects the spinal cord (para. 2). It is easier to have the energy to be a change agent if I am making healthy food choices.

This fuel gives me more energy to exercise. I exercise because I want to say "thank you" to my body. I am grateful for a body that allows me to accomplish many tasks and reminds me when I need to take a break or stretch. Mandel (2009) writes, "Exercise helps us to restore focus and decompress, to return to ourselves and find balance in an unstable medium" (p. 44). Life is busy, stressful, and unpredictable. Exercise, whether a walk around my neighborhood or a cardio workout, allows me to take a break and tend to myself in a way that helps me gain perspective.

Mind

Social workers and other helping professionals spend a great deal of time thinking. We also spend time learning. Part of professional practice involves staying abreast of current events and up-to-date professional knowledge. Also, time spent with individuals, families, groups, communities, and co-workers is time that the mind is engaged and active. Just like the body, the mind needs balance. When our minds are overworked or unbalanced, we are being a disservice to ourselves and others. Wicks and Buck (2013) remind us, "Professionals need to take responsibility for leading balanced lives. They must strive to be physically healthy, emotionally alive, and intellectually curious" (p. 4).

In our culture, a plethora of information is available to be consumed. I must be judicious in my consumption, or I can be easily overwhelmed. I "feed" my mind with a wide range of materials. If I have been reading professional literature for an extended period of time, or have been bombarded with media that tends to focus on violence or negativity, I will take time to listen to music or watch a funny video. I also try to balance my "information" with inspiration—which feeds my spirit. As well, I balance my intake of information with plenty of rest and meditation. Taking a nap or taking slow, deep breaths are ways I give my mind some "down time" so that it can have a break. This balance keeps me more refreshed, so when I am consuming information, I am able to digest it more critically and effectively.

Spirit

My spirit is the reason I am passionate about social work. I find it helpful to remember that what I am choosing to "feed" myself spiritually will guide how I am of service to others. My spirituality is the foundation for my thoughts, deeds, and actions. I am inspired by many things like nature, photography, a well-written story, a peaceful song, a good laugh, and many other spiritually fulfilling items. It is important, for each of us, to find what creates peace, serenity, and joy in spirit.

I am a human being, and I can draw from my spiritual experience to give to others, without depleting myself. We are living in a world with unprecedented access to the global community. This admission into the lives of so many people touches that place in me that desires to help. I must remember that I am a member of the global community, but I am not solely responsible for the community. My spiritual principles guide me to serve but remind me that the universe is a vast place, and something much larger than me is running the show.

Conclusion

No matter if the self-care you are practicing is related to mind, body, and/or spirit, it is important for the action to give instead of take from the body. I must care for myself so I will have the energy to give to others. Wicks and Buck (2013) summarized this concept nicely:

> And this effort is not simply about their personal welfare—as important as it is. Their sense of peace and a healthy perspective are among the greatest attributes they can share with those they supervise or treat, but they cannot share what they do not have. (pp. 4-5)

It is my responsibility to "feed" my mind, body, and spirit with substance that allows for both nurturing and growth.

I believe that professional helpers are in a prime position to model desirable actions and behaviors to the rest of the world. When I am well "fed" in body, mind, and spirit, then I am a better social worker and, more importantly, a better human being. It is not always easy to care for myself every hour of every day. However, intentional self-care practices offer me a guide that makes it easier. Please, "feed" your mind, body, and spirit with whatever gives you energy, peace, and good health. Have a daily diet that replenishes, restores, and renews.

Reflection/Discussion

1. Think about your daily "diet." How do you "feed" your body, mind, and spirit?
2. What are some SMART ways you could change your eating and exercise habits?
3. Consider your balance in regard to your intake of information. How do you achieve that balance, or how might you achieve it? What is the relationship between your spirit and your professional practice? Consider how those aspects are connected or disconnected and how you might incorporate spirituality as a part of your self-care.

Selected Resources

Centers for Disease Control and Prevention. (n.d.). *Water & Nutrition.* Retrieved from *http://www.cdc.gov/healthywater/ drinking/nutrition/*

Mandel, D. (2005). Small steps, giant gains in self-care. *Social Work Today, 5*(6), 44-46.

Wicks, R. J., & Buck, T. C. (2013). Riding the dragon: Enhancing resilient leadership and sensible self-care in the health-care executive. *Frontiers of Health Services Management, 30*(2), 3-13.

Exercise: Fantastic 4 Fitness Foundations
Elena Winburn

Have you ever felt so stressed that you just wanted to close the blinds and stay in bed? I have! Stress affects us physically and psychologically. It can decrease our productivity and steal bright colors from our world. It can impair our critical thinking skills and wipe the smile off our faces. Stress does not have to rule our lives and actions. Multiple tools can be used to deal with stress.

Exercising Self-Care

Exercise is a key protective factor against the harmful effects of stress, and it is an essential part of any self-care plan. Daily, we hear about the positive benefits of physical activity on our overall well-being. For example, Hassmen, Koivula, and Uutela (2000) identified exercise as a positive behavior with multiple benefits for human well-being. People who exercise at least two times a week are significantly less depressed, angry, and stressed. Physically active individuals experience stronger feelings of social acceptance. And these are only a few examples of the positive impacts of exercise.

Yet, do we really implement this effective tool in our lives? According to the Centers for Disease Control and Prevention (2014), only about one in five Americans meet the 2008 physical activity guidelines. If you are a person who regularly exercises and leads an active lifestyle, I admire that you are a person of discipline; you may want to skip to the next entry and go to the gym instead. However, if you are like me, and staying active is a challenge, then, welcome to this section of the book.

Physical exercise can be an "easy" routine; yet, it is one of the most challenging "chores" we try to avoid. We have plenty of excuses not to go for a walk with the dog or sign up for a yoga class (often citing the lack of time). We may say we do not feel good and spend the rest of the evening on the couch. When we stress, we feel tired and, therefore, it seems logical to rest and avoid physical activities. Despite what we may know regarding positive effects of exercise, we avoid doing what's right for us.

In this entry, I hope to identify effective strategies for combating everyday stress through exercise. We can incorporate exercise into our daily life. However, I found that the fewer guidelines, the easier it is for me to follow them.

Fantastic 4 Fitness Foundations

So, let me introduce you to an approach I call my Fantastic 4 Fitness Foundations. I found that four steps are enough to develop a strong and consistent routine! You can be creative and add (or subtract) exercise strategies. Have your own Fantastic 5 or Terrific 2. Adapt and make it work just for you. The goal is not to become a professional athlete, but, rather, a healthy adult who effectively incorporates exercise to manage stress.

Fitness Foundation One: You're the Captain of your ship. Or, put another way, you are your own coach.

Certainly, you may choose to consult with a personal trainer, if that fits your style. But really, no one can tell you what exercise works best for you. You know how your body operates and how it reacts to stress. If jogging works for your friend, it does not mean it will work for you.

Ask yourself two main questions: Does jogging make you feel good? Do you enjoy this type of exercise? If the answer is "no," then look for a different routine. The world is full of fun things. Look for something that you enjoy doing. Be creative. You don't have to perform boring exercises. If you don't enjoy doing something, it will be extremely hard to be consistent.

For example, I enjoy exercising in summer. My physical routine consists of gardening during this wonderful season. Surprised? Gardening can be great for releasing stress (only if you enjoy gardening, of course). The acts of pulling weeds, plowing, and picking delicious crops bring so much joy into my life and exercise my body at the same time. Explore your interests and find what works for you!

Fitness Foundation Two: Start your day in bed.

How many times have you proclaimed that you absolutely have no time for physical activity in the morning? Mornings are the hardest for me. I often feel unrested and sleepy. My first thought is how to make my way to the coffee machine—my personal fatigue fix! I do not care if this energy potion (a.k.a. coffee) works just for a few hours and then its magical power wears off. I make coffee instead of exercising, because it is easier. It does not require too much effort from me; all I have to do is to press buttons. Therefore, I am seeking easier—not better—ways. Easy does not mean effective.

What if I told you that you can exercise without leaving your bed in the morning? You can do multiple exercises in your own bed (e.g., Munson, 2014; Reynolds, 2013). I do some simple stretches before getting out of bed and while I wait for my coffee to brew. They are easy, effective, and fun. This morning routine helps start my day with an energy boost, mood lifter, and sense of accomplishment.

I invite you to try this Fitness Foundation. Do a web search for exercises/stretches that appeal to you. Your body will need a couple of weeks to adjust to the new ritual, so don't expect immediate results.

Fitness Foundation Three: Stand up for yourself! Kiss the chair good-bye! Live a little longer!

Inactivity for people is not only unwise, but it is also against human nature (Reynolds, 2012). It can bring not only unhealthy extra weight, but also contributes to life-threatening diseases. Such a statement creates a powerful message for me. I don't want to die earlier because my work encourages a sedentary lifestyle. I am curious about this world. I want to learn new things, experience a wide range of emotions, and acquire new skills. I want to raise my children and watch them grow, graduate, and possibly get married. I might not be able to do it if I succumb to cruel effects of stress, spending my life "motionless."

Therefore, all we have to do is sit less and move more! Standing is better than sitting. Any chair can be our enemy, because it promotes a sedentary lifestyle. It assists us in accumulating stress in our bodies and prevents us from walking out our stress (e.g., Dalkilinc, n.d.). Sometimes it is hard to avoid a chair at work or home, but here is a way.

I practice what I call my "walkie-talkie" strategy. For example, when wanting to talk to my family members about a stressful day, I suggest we go for a walk outside. My husband and I can put our baby in the stroller and take a 20-minute walk while debriefing about the day. Or, when I talk on the phone, I try to stand up from the chair and pace around the room or take a walk. Even at work, instead of sitting in meetings (especially with only one or two others), incorporate walks around the building or outside—walkie-talkie meetings. Five minutes here and there contributes to becoming a more active person.

Try being a "walkie-talkie." By the end of the day, you won't feel so guilty for sitting on the chair or a couch all day. You will feel better for taking 5-minute walkie-talkie breaks. Every small step is a rebellion against stress attack!

Fitness Foundation Four: Wish Upon an App

Since we live in a world full of technology gadgets, you can make your smartphone (if you have one) work for you. Multiple apps are available to assist people in tracking their steps, counting calorie intake, and even monitoring heart rate and quality of sleep. If you don't have a smartphone, you can always find a specialized watch that will do all these tricks for you. Or, utilize a FitBit or pedometer.

Why might this strategy work? Although you are your own coach, an easy activity tracking app can become your trusty personal assistant who will not exaggerate, lie, or cover up for you. If you made 200 steps during a day (when your daily goal was set at 5,000), your "assistant" will tell you that fact, without feeling bad for you or making excuses!

Good diet, exercise, and healthy sleep are basic factors that help you be an effective helping professional and happy human being. Exercising is a habit that needs to be maintained. Just remember, it is up to you to combat stress effectively, but you are not alone on this journey. Small changes can lead to great achievements. (See *Kaizen Method* entry.) Give the Fantastic 4 Fitness Foundations a chance. Experiment! Have fun! If something doesn't fit your style, find another Fantastic way that Fits you. Exercise your right to choose—but regardless, EXERCISE!

Reflection/Discussion

1. I dubbed my exercise approach the Fantastic 4 Fitness Foundations. What might you call your exercise plan? What aspects would you incorporate?
2. What are the smallest, SMARTest steps you could take toward your own personalized exercise plan?

Selected Resources

Centers for Disease Control and Prevention. (2014). *Physical activity.* Retrieved April 12, 2015 from *http://www.cdc.gov/physicalactivity/data/facts.htm*

Dalkilinc, M. (n.d.) Why sitting is bad for you. Retrieved April 12, 2015 from *http://ed.ted.com/lessons/why-sitting-is-bad-for-you-murat-dalkilinc*

Hassmen, P., Koivula, N., & Uutela, A. (2000). Physical exercise and psychological well-being: A population study in Finland. *Preventive Medicine. 30*(1), 17-25.

Munson, R. (2014). *12 Ab-toning exercises you can do in bed (that actually work).* Retrieved April 12, 2015 from *http://www.marieclaire.co.uk/blogs/545904/12-ab-toning-exercises-you-can-do-in-bed-that-actually-work.html*

Reynolds, G. (2013). *The first 20 minutes: Surprising science reveals how we can exercise better, train smarter, live longer.* London, England: Icon Books Ltd.

"F" Word: Fear
Tabitha DeLeon

Our deepest fear is not that we are inadequate. Our deepest fear is that we are powerful beyond measure. It is our light, not our darkness, that most frightens us....

Marianne Williamson, from *A Return to Love*

This line from the poem entitled *Our Deepest Fear,* by Marianne Williamson (1992), accurately explains the true nature of our fears. What we fear most originates from a feeling of unworthiness, shame, guilt, and doubt. We are afraid to be who we truly are because of our fears of inadequacy and unworthiness. We fear judgment, isolation, and not being accepted.

What Does Fear Have to Do with Self-Care?

Our thought process (i.e., "self-talk") directly affects our attention to self-care. Think about any of the self-care strategies you might want to undertake and any impediment to that self-care. Typically, at root, fear is a significant impediment. For instance, you may want to set healthier boundaries with your work life and in your personal life. At first, you may attribute the barrier to external demands or expectations. But, most likely, you are afraid of not being liked, respected, or rewarded.

Oprah Winfrey (2014) said that fear can immobilize us, if we let it (p. 103). She describes how she spent a year journaling about the question: *What am I afraid of?* Like many of us, she learned that her fears kept her locked in unhealthy habits and blocked her joy—even amidst extraordinary success and wealth. Her fears were crystallized in wanting to please others and wanting to always be liked.

It wasn't until I spent focused time asking, "What am I afraid of?" that I discovered my core fear. I feared being unworthy and incapable of success, happiness, and good fortune of any kind. I was afraid of my own abilities and capacity. I began realizing that I was the sum of the expectations, thoughts, and judgments enforced on me by peers, family, and society. This fear was so ingrained that I had no idea that "who I was" was *not* who I *actually* was at all but instead who I was told to be and expected to be by everyone else around me.

> *...We ask ourselves, who am I to be brilliant, gorgeous, talented and fabulous? Actually, who are you not to be? You are a child of God. Your playing small does not serve the world. There's nothing enlightened about shrinking so that other people won't feel insecure around you....* (Williamson, 1992)

So, Now What? (Don't Be Afraid to Ask!)

In her poem, Williamson goes on to proclaim that we are all unique, talented, and brilliant individuals in our own right. Everyone is beautiful and fabulous, and everyone has a right to be. When we become preoccupied with the opinions of others, we begin to doubt ourselves, feel less than, or become trapped in the process of trying to make decisions with the thoughts and opinions of others in our mind.

But how do we release ourselves from these fears and limiting beliefs? A first step, which is usually the hardest—acknowledgment—comes through identifying what we are afraid of, which requires honest and intentional reflection.

Maclean (2011) writes that reflection is essential for ongoing professional development and self-care. Reflection allows the time, space, and opportunity to consider our experiences and how we have internalized them, the associated feelings, consequences, reactions, and other outcomes. Overcoming fear is not an easy or instant process. It takes a continuous, conscious effort over time to make a lasting change. Learning from our experiences requires reflection. Deep learning that changes us is transformative. Mezirow and Associates (2000) outline 10 steps in transformative learning:

1. experience something disorienting;
2. examine personal thoughts and beliefs;

3/4. assess assumptions and the alienation created by challenging these assumptions;

5. explore various options for new ways of acting;

6/7. plan a course of action and begin to acquire the knowledge and develop the skills required for the action;

8. test out new behaviors and skills, seek and use feedback;

9. build confidence and competence in new approach; and

10. re-integrate with a new perspective (p. 22).

Jaimal Yogis (2013), journalist and surfer, embarked on a "Fear Project," in which he explored his own experiences with fear and synthesized interviews with an intriguing array of informants, such as neuroscientists, spiritual gurus, and professional athletes. In his book, he articulates how much power fear has in our life experiences, but how little is understood about it. So, mirroring the steps for transformative learning, his first recommendation is to intentionally learn about fear. He clarifies that fear is an experience, based on our interpretations. (As Will Smith's character in the movie *After Earth* observed: "Danger is very real, but fear is a choice.") Thus, Yogis suggests practices such as using mindfulness, reframing fear, and harnessing fear as fuel to have healthier interpretations and, thus, responses. Providing an impressive range of information and useful suggestions, Yogis concluded that the antidote to fear is love.

What's Love Got to Do with It?

Our fears manifest in our thoughts and actions. In developing a deeper understanding of my fear, I realized that it manifested as an avoidance of commitment, along with a fear of the unknown and situations I could not control. If I did not commit to something or someone, then I could not become attached. No attachment or commitment meant no expectations, no disappointment, no betrayal, no abandonment, no hurt. It has been a long time coming, but I have realized, through personal experience and reflection, the beauty that comes with facing my fear of commitment. Authenticity and intimacy can only be achieved by committing to be present, thoughtful, and genuinely engaged in relationships with other people. When my fear comes in, it builds walls rather than healthy boundaries; it blocks my vulnerability that allows me to be seen by other people—and even by myself.

Remaining in a fearful state only keeps these walls up and keeps me imprisoned. It is challenging to let down walls, because I cannot control the final outcome and am unsure if it will result in love, friendship, betrayal, or distrust. But I know for sure that not letting them down will 100% of the time result in negative outcomes, such as feelings of isolation, resentment, shame, and guilt. Letting down these walls of fear opens me up for the possibility to experience trust, companionship, friendship, and intimacy. Certainly, it may still result in negative outcomes and feelings, but I have learned that my odds are better on the other side of the wall. Bad experiences are not failures; they are experience, our greatest teacher. They can serve to add knowledge and reference points in future experiences.

When it comes right down to the core, fear is the antithesis of love. Major religions and philosophies teach this core principle (e.g., *John 4:18*—*"Perfect love casts out fear").* One cannot exist in the presence of the other. Both involve choices we perpetuate in our thoughts and actions. If you are operating from fear, you cannot unconditionally love yourself and others. We cannot truly understand, care, and love others until we have taken the time to do so for ourselves. *Being* and engaging in the world free from fear, from a position of love, gives others courage to do the same.

> *...And as we let our own light shine, we unconsciously give other people permission to do the same. As we are liberated from our own fear, our presence automatically liberates others.* (Williamson, 1992)

Reflection/Discussion

1. What do you think about the relationship between fear (and other negative self-talk) and self-care? What do you think about the statement that love is the antithesis of fear?
2. Consider the reflection exercise described on page 47. What are you afraid of? What are two of your biggest fears? What are some specific ideas and strategies to help cope with these fears?
3. How does fear make you feel? Think about your body's responses internally and externally.
4. Think of your most significant accomplishments in life thus far. What did it take to make it happen? What were the fears that impeded you? Think about strategies, thoughts, attitudes, and habits that were helpful in overcoming these fears. How can you apply those same aspects to a current or future goal?

Selected Resources

Maclean, S. (2011). *The social work pocket guide to...stress and burnout.* Lichfield, Staffordshire, England: Kirwin Maclean Associates LTD.

Meizrow, J. & Associates (2000). *Learning as transformation.* San Francisco, CA: Jossey-Bass.

Williamson, M. (1992). *Our deepest fear.* In *A return to love: Reflections on the principles of a course in miracles.* New York, NY: HarperCollins.

Winfrey, O. (2014). *What I know for sure.* New York, NY: FlatIron Books.

Yogis, J. (2013). *The fear project: What our most primal emotion taught me about survival, success, surfing...and love.* New York, NY: Rodale.

Gratitude: Walking the Path With Appreciation

Tammy L. Quetot

As a military social worker, I am privileged to work with the families of fallen soldiers. Every day, I deal with death, despair, and discouragement. Of course, I also encounter courage, hope, and resilience. I know that self-care is essential for staying healthy and balanced.

Along the Way

About a year ago, I discovered that I was living life like an amateur mountain climber. I felt stuck in the middle of my journey, hanging from a cliff and out of supplies. Hanging there, I wished I had chosen to walk the paths and parks that lay at the foot of the mountain. Then it occurred to me: *When I get to where I am going, am I really there?* The answer was, "No!" I was so worried about what lay ahead and in such a hurry to get there, that I was not living in the NOW! I found myself constantly worrying about decisions I had made in the past and the destinations ahead, rather than being grateful for where I was.

When we find ourselves living in the present, gratitude emerges, and we discover the full experience of what is in front of us. Out of a cliff-hanging crisis, I began a journey of discovery. Come walk with me as I share how I am discovering how to live life with gratitude as a guide.

I truly believe everything happens for a reason. Every experience offers lessons in life and can teach us to never take anything for granted. Have you ever noticed that when expressing gratitude to someone, the recipient's expression, body language, and mood change? Gratitude makes us feel good inside—and it is reflected externally. We gain the full attention of others when we show gratitude toward them. We, as humans, truly have a passageway through to another's soul when sharing gratitude. Gratitude touches another person's soul. Likewise, it is a way to move our own soul.

Two Paths: Doom and Bloom

Imagine a choice of two paths. Each path holds a sign. One sign is bent and rusty and holds the faded word "Doom." Looking down the path, notice overgrown, dead foliage. Sunlight cannot seep through the gloomy overgrowth. The dreary sounds of wilted dry leaves and decay rattle in the wind.

The other sign is mounted tall; it gleams in the sunlight with the word "Bloom." Down this path, notice green fields of grass, liberally sprinkled with wild flowers saturated in the sunshine. Hear the cheerful songs of birds and the buzzing sounds of nature's heartbeat.

We all have a choice of which path to take. Certainly, we can all wish that we would choose the positive path, regardless of circumstances. But, sometimes, we allow curiosity or discouragement or other sirens to get the best of us. Before we know it, we are heading in the wrong direction. At these times, we need to pause, be thankful for our experiences, and find the lesson at hand. Going down either path, we can recognize that we have become stronger and wiser. Then, gratitude comes to walk alongside us.

Write This Way

On our path, gratitude can serve as a guide. Brené Brown (2010) emphasizes that "whole-hearted" people do not merely have an "attitude of gratitude." Rather, they *practice* gratitude in an active way.

One of the ways I practice gratitude is through my gratitude journal. This practice helps me stay focused and reminds me of my blessings each day. I bought a basic journal at a local bookstore and enhanced it with personal touches from my craft and scrapbooking supplies. This enhancement made it more meaningful and personal.

I strive to write an entry once a day. I allow myself some quiet time to reflect on the day, review my journal, and write an entry. I use different categories to both structure and personalize my reflections. Here are some of the categories my journal holds:

- My Triggers of Joy
- My Passions
- Primary Components of My Happiness
- Positive Outcomes to Negative Situations
- Awesome, I AM
- Encouragement for My Soul
- 10 Favorite Memories
- Accomplishments and Contributions
- Unexpected, Great Things and Surprises
- Ah ha! Moments – I see why
- Sense versus Nonsense

For instance, when I write entries in my journal under "Sense versus Nonsense," I apply critical thinking to situations in which I am second-guessing or doubting myself. Here is an entry I have written as an affirmation to myself— and it incorporates my love of horseback riding. Under the column titled *Sense,* I wrote, "I must ride my horse through this current storm and splash through each mud puddle placed before me." Under the column titled *Nonsense,* I wrote "I will never dismount and sit in a puddle or get stuck in the mud." I keep my entries simple so I can, in a glance, use it as a quick guide for encouragement on my life journey.

Pebbles of Affirmations

Paths oftentimes have rocks that serve to pave the way or can be painful probes. I like the creative use of writing positive words on stones. In that spirit, I use metaphorical pebbles of affirmation to evoke gratitude on my path. Throughout my week, these affirmations serve to silence the critic within. I incorporate these affirmations in various ways, such as apps on my iPhone. One of my favorites is *Affirmations* by Michael Quach (2014). This app has 365 inspiring quotes. Sometimes in life, we cross paths with negative people or situations and find ourselves being "pulled down" by them. We can find ourselves being drawn into their drama or negativity. Having this app at my fingertips reminds me of the person I truly am and encourages reflection on my authentic self and the blessings of each day.

Another of my favorite tools for affirmations is Dyer's (1995) *Staying On the Path*. The book measures 4x4 inches, and each page is slightly larger than a Post-it note. The size allows me to tear out a page and post affirmations on my bathroom mirror, car dashboard, around the office, and share with family and friends.

No matter the path, with gratitude as a guide, we can have much more awareness of how wonderful life is. Our decisions and thoughts influence how we feel and perceive life. Gratitude can be felt, shown, shared, spoken, written, and witnessed. I am learning to reframe my thinking and become aware of my thought patterns. I encourage you to learn to recognize when you are not feeling or sharing gratitude. And, more importantly, learn what works for you in practicing gratitude. It can be as simple as developing a habit of stopping to say: "I am grateful for...."

Always allow yourself to accept gratitude from others, savor that moment and carry it with you. Allow it to become an echo when you are feeling discouraged. Develop the best strategies that will help you live in the NOW and remind you of the greatness and goodness that life holds in all situations. When we are present, we have a better view and can focus on what is in front of us...and let gratitude be our guide.

Reflection/Discussion

1. What do you think about gratitude's role in self-care? What have been your experiences with gratitude and its effects on your well-being?
2. What are three things you are grateful for today?
3. Think of someone you have wanted to express gratitude toward, but have put it off. Consider taking the time today to express that gratitude, either directly or indirectly.

4. Think of a time when someone expressed gratitude toward you. What was it that made you think of this particular time?

5. I use a gratitude journal and affirmations to support my commitment to practicing gratitude. What are some ways that you could begin or enhance using "gratitude as a guide" on your path?

Selected Resources

Brown, B. (2010). *The gifts of imperfection: Let go of who you think you're supposed to be and embrace who you are.* Center City, MN: Hazelden.

Dyer, W. W. (1995). *Staying on the path.* Carlsbad, CA: Hay House, Inc.

Quach, M. (2014). Affirmations! Daily self-esteem help solutions and life improvement complete guide: The positive thinking affirmation tips and secrets for key success and happiness (Version 2.2.4). [Mobile Application Software]. Retrieved from *https://itunes.apple.com/us/app/affirmations!/id328011102?mt=8*

Humor: Participating in Life's Awarding opportunitY (PLAY)
Ana'neicia Williams

My days at work are long and dreadful when no humor or play is involved. So, I have declared myself the "CEO (Chief *Enjoyment* Officer) of PLAY." I am the co-worker who makes it my duty to make you smile or laugh. Whether telling one of my many knock-knock jokes or discussing the latest celebrities' red carpet disasters, I ensure I laugh regularly, even if at myself. Laughing at myself serves as a reminder that I am human. I'm going to make mistakes. I won't know everything, and I do not have to take things so literally and seriously all the time.

Self-Care: Practice Rule #6

Zander and Zander (2000) tell the story of a conversation between two prime ministers being interrupted multiple times by angry, hysterical complainants. The resident prime minister achieves instant good humor and calmness in each instance by reminding the complainants to "Remember Rule #6." Intrigued, the visiting prime minister asks, "What is this Rule #6?" The resident prime minister clarifies, "It's simple: Don't take yourself so seriously!" The visitor inquires, "What are the other rules?" The response: "Oh, there aren't any!"

Rule #6 is a good one for self-care! Because of the important work we do, we can take ourselves too seriously. Many of us have forgotten how to play since coming into the adulthood stage. We have been trained that we're too old to play—we shall behave the way of adults. (I'm still trying to figure out exactly what way that is!) As we know, there is no handbook on adult behavior and how we should act. So take the pressure off yourself! In fact, make it a point to play at work, home, and everyday life. Play and humor have no age requirements!

Did you know that humor and play are related to a healthy lifestyle? When people make play and humor part of their lives, they are healthier and happier. Benefits include relieving stress, improving brain function, connecting with others, improving mental health, and increasing energy (Public Broadcasting Service, n.d.).

Play and humor are essential for self-care! What could be more important than play for preventing burnout? To learn more about the benefits of play, check out the National Institute for Play (n.d.), founded by Dr. Stuart Brown, who wrote *Play: How it Shapes the Brain, Opens the Imagination, and Invigorates the Soul* (2009).

Humor Me: Hard Work Requires More Play!

Humans have such a tendency to consume our lives with work that we can exclude enjoying the work that we are doing. I found myself to be doing that with my current employment. Upon reflection, I realized I needed to find some coping skills that would allow me to manage my stressful job.

When I first started this job, I found it very difficult to adjust to the pace and population with whom I worked. I assist children who come from a low socioeconomic status. Many have learning disabilities, behavioral issues, and mental illnesses. Most are from families with generational poverty. These factors can be overwhelming. I had to find ways to make those tough work days more enjoyable.

So, I promised myself at least 30 minutes of play time each day. I promised myself I would giggle, grin, or smile at least every hour. Otherwise, I would not survive. To hold myself accountable, I involved my co-workers. After shifts, I sit down with my co-workers and engage in conversation. We share the highs and lows of our day. We vent about which kids we hope won't attend the next day so we can re-group. Even in the difficult times, we all manage to laugh about what had us ready to put in our resignation hours ago. To cope, we joke about someone's day worse off than ours; we can laugh at them and with them.

I can easily incorporate play at work. Working with kids, they always want to play a game. Engaging in a card/board game or an infamous dodgeball game provides me the opportunity to connect with others and simply be a kid again. Expanding this sense of play with co-workers extends the benefits for all of us.

Participate in Life's Awarding opportunitY

You've heard it before: "All work and no play..." leads one's life to dullness. Brown (2009) even contends that the opposite of play is not work—it is depression! Luckily, I am in a position where my job incorporates play. Play is rejuvenating, invigorating, and just fun! Rubin (2009) says that researchers define play as any activity that's inherently satisfying, has no economic significance, doesn't create social harm, and doesn't necessarily lead to praise or recognition. If you struggle with ways to incorporate play or don't have the opportunity at your work, I have some ideas for you.

For the Parent (or Any Adult). Children tend to keep us young at heart. Even if you do not have kids, "borrow" your niece or nephew, grandchild, little cousin—kids are everywhere! Take the opportunity to use a child as your excuse to be a kid again. Whether playing a board game, going to the park, or just simply having the company of a child, you can find humor, play, and fun.

For the Workaholic. Find time outside of work to meet up with colleagues for dinner, bowling, or some type of outing that allows you to interact with them. As I have described, commit to incorporating play at work—not just after work.

For the Student. Disconnect from your phone and social media for a week. Take time to explore parks in your neighborhood and community. Invite friends and play a game of kickball, Frisbee, or Hide and Seek.

You cannot always expect humor and play to come and find you. Sometimes you have to make it a priority to seek it, invite it, and invent it! It is said that you use more muscles frowning than smiling. So, encourage yourself to laugh even if it's by yourself. Humor and play can be done anywhere, with very little cost!

When it comes to play: **P**articipate in **L**ife's **A**warding opportunit**Y.** We remind ourselves of appointments and upcoming events. So, why not make it a priority to put some humor and play into your day? Humor and play can be essential if you allow yourself to be exposed. As the "CEO of PLAY," I now give you permission to schedule your humor and play in advance. Make it part of your job description, and make it part of your life's goals. You will find it PLAYS wonderful dividends in your health and happiness. And, in a parallel play process, this PLAY approach can have an impact on our work with clients (Klein, 2010). So, PLAY it forward.

Reflection/Discussion

1. How can you take the time to consciously and effectively integrate humor into your life?
2. What challenges you from being able to add humor and play into your everyday routine?
3. What are some of the activities you engage in that make you laugh?
4. Think about your workplace. How might you incorporate more humor and play into the everyday?

Selected Resources

Brown, S. (with Vaughan, C.) (2009). *Play: How it shapes the brain, opens the imagination, and invigorates the soul.* New York, NY: Penguin Group.

Klein, A. (2010). *L.A.U.G.H.: Using humor and play to help clients cope with stress, anger, frustration, and more.* Plainview, NY: Wellness Reproductions and Publishing, Inc.

National Institute for Play. (n.d.). Retrieved from *http://www.nifplay.org/institute/about-us/*

Public Broadcasting Service. (n.d.). Benefits of humor. Retrieved from *http://www.pbs.org/thisemotionallife/topic/humor/benefits-humor*

Rubin, G. (2009). *The happiness project: Or, why I spent a year trying to sing in the morning, clean my closets, fight right, read Aristotle, and generally have more fun.* New York, NY: HarperCollins.

Zander, R. S., & Zander, B. (2000). *The art of possibility: Transforming professional and personal life.* New York, NY: Penguin Books.

Individualized: Throw Yourself a Party of One
Stacey Sougoufara

Imagine throwing yourself a party. Select a venue, décor, and theme. You are planning something special just for you. How would your personal invitation read? This party is like no other. It's a party of one—that can happen as often as you like. Material gifts may or may not be necessary, depending on preference. However, the main gift is the individualized approach you take to designing a self-care plan.

Party Planning and Self-Care Plans: The "I"s Have It!

Individualized self-care plans are necessary for those working in the helping profession. Like planning a party, drafting a self-care plan requires thoughtful consideration of your needs and wishes. What gift should you provide? Giving so much to others (professional or personal) can be draining. You need some "I" time! Here are some *"I"*s for an individualized self-care plan: Identify Immediate Intentional Interventions and Invest!

First, *identify* what self-care means to you. How an individual identifies needs is a unique experience. So ask yourself: *What is my main concern?* For many, a list of concerns will surface. For others, identifying that one thing that causes uneasiness will be obvious. However, it is important to START small. Because we live in a society that grooms us to think BIG, dream BIG, and live BIG, we often struggle with thinking small. As adults, we have numerous obligations and commitments, which often involve others. A self-care plan involves YOU, the individual. Remember, you know what you want. So, starting small becomes beneficial. (See *Kaizen* entry.)

Take time to narrow down the concern that is MOST important. Which concern requires *immediate* attention? This process will cause you to prioritize. For example, your initial concern list might read: lose weight, sleep 6-8 hours at night, decrease work stress and financial concerns. At first glance, all listed are important. However, targeting the most important is not only more realistic; it will afford an opportunity to experience immediate results, which is encouraging. Feeling better, thinking more clearly, and getting what we want motivates us to continue with successful interventions and attainable goals.

Self-care requires *intentional intervention.* What are you able to commit to routinely that will address your concern? These commitments may include a bubble bath on Friday nights, an evening walk following dinner, or a structured activity like a yoga class twice a week. Intentional intervention is a commitment that you adhere to in order to reach your self-care goals.

Additional interventions and goals may follow, after your initial self-care plan is in place. For example, an evening walk after dinner during the week may be so satisfying that you add a morning walk after breakfast on Saturdays. Oftentimes, our goals are more apparent than the interventions (or level of required involvement). Although we want what we want, we are each responsible for results. Parties—especially parties for one—do not happen without intentional attention.

Finally, an effective self-care plan requires *investment.* A good party requires thinking through needed resources and potential obstacles and being willing to put in the effort needed to make it a success. Although some may "succeed" on the first attempt, others may have to revise individualized self-care plans. Don't fret if this revision happens to you. Remember, you are an individual, and so are your needs.

It's YOUR Party—Do YOUR Thing!

I have edited my self-care plan multiple times. After multiple attempts, revisions, and facing obstacles, I finally drafted a plan that works for me. Here was the main problem I faced: I was invited (with kind intent) to apply everyone else's self-care plan. As I reviewed my track record of unsuccessful "parties," I quickly realized that I was not approaching my needs as an individual. Whew! Something had to give!

After months of trial and error, my objective became clear. Using my brand new notepad, I listed concerns. As in past attempts, the concern remained the same: health and wellness. Prior to this attempt, I tried suggested self-care plans, such as walking in the park with my friends, crash diets, and a gym membership. Nothing worked. Careful review of my lack of "success" revealed two factors: (1) I didn't find enjoyment in any of the above activities, and (2) I placed my family's needs before my own.

What was I suggesting to myself and others by participating in activities that I didn't enjoy and placing myself last on the list of importance? Reflecting on this question helped me realize that I am just as important as my family, their activities, and their commitments. The need to position myself as a priority was an important step toward developing my self-care plan. Although initially a struggle, I overcame feeling awkward about my new position: *first.*

First position required me to campaign for myself. My 8-year-old daughter was quite amused when I announced that I was making a commitment to health and wellness. Surprisingly, she is my biggest supporter. After careful review, I determined that joining a local 6-week boot camp would give me the structure and enjoyment I needed. Psychologist Carl Rogers (as cited in Myers, 1999) noted, "The only question which matters is, am I living in a way which is deeply satisfying to me, and which truly expresses me?" (p. 248). So, I called the trainer, obtained a schedule, showed up, and worked out.

Although I make it sound easy, it hasn't been. But I finally found a perfect fit. I work out three times a week for a rigorous hour. Building on this initial change, I now follow a strict meal plan and have developed a support system with a cohort of eight women. Nothing prohibits me from attending class. Every class, I'm there, on time, and ready to PARTY, a.k.a. work out!

Following the first class, I experienced immediate results. My concentration and energy level increased. My sleep improved. These immediate results were the encouragement I needed to continue. For now, boot camp is the central part of my self-care plan. This plan is simple for me.

Remember, even though planning a party, keep things simple. In time, revising or reviewing your self-care plan will be apparent. For me, checking in when needed works best. Knowing that I am making progress is rewarding. Even small rewards make excellent gifts.

Following through with a solid self-care plan takes dedication and discipline. These are leadership characteristics. For me, I realize that my daughter is watching closely; she is aware of my health and wellness campaign. She attends boot camp with me by her choice and always tells me how proud she is of me. In turn, I am teaching her that health and wellness are attainable and that my needs are just as important as anyone else's.

There will always be more to do and more to "fix." There is no need to address all of your concerns at once. Start small and add on as you go. Compose your plan your way.

Do your thing! In planning your party, how will the invitation read?

Your party theme is what you're most concerned about and your intervention to address it. The date and time is your routine, how often and when it will take place. The venue is simply the place. Remember, it's a party for one. Party time!

Reflection/Discussion

1. How can you make your party/self-care plan individualized? What would your personalized invitation say?
2. What would your *"I"*s look like: Identify Immediate Intentional Interventions and Invest?
3. If you already have a self-care plan, what revisions might make it more YOUR THING?

Selected Resources

Myers, D. (1999). *Social psychology.* Boston, MA: McGraw-Hill.

Rogers, C. (1961). *On becoming a person.* Boston, MA: Houghton Mifflin.

Job Satisfaction—Finding Joy in Your Work
Kaniktra Steadmon & Andrea Russell

What one person thinks in terms of job satisfaction will very likely vary somewhat from the next person. A 2013 survey showed 81% of United States employees are over-all satisfied with their jobs (Society for Human Resource Management, 2014). In this survey, 60% identified financial compensation as a "very important" factor. As social work-ers, financial compensation is not the top reason we have chosen to be helping professionals (although we deserve fair and just compensation for the important work we do!) We also did not choose social work primarily because of job security, low stress levels, and lavish benefits.

Many of us would say social work is our "calling." We are in this field to improve the lives of others, make a differ-ence, bring social justice, and change the world. But, with the psychological strain of the profession, how do we con-tinue to be satisfied with what we do? How do we keep the passion in the work we love? We have found the answer is self-care—not just away from work, but in our work. In this entry, we discuss ways we implement self-care practice to increase job satisfaction.

Social Connectedness

While being interviewed for the social work program at Spalding University, one of the authors (Andrea) stated, "I like things to be black and white, because I don't like gray areas." The interviewer responded, "Maybe you should consider being an engineer, because social work is all about gray areas." Later, at orientation, the MSW director said students might enter the MSW program seeing the world in black and white, but she hoped we would leave it seeing the world in technicolor. Oftentimes, no right or wrong is absolute when dealing with people and the complexity of the problems they face.

In this technicolor, complex world, helping professionals often find it difficult to know whether they have made the right decision with a client, given the best advice, or if they have been patient enough. During these times, we must rely on support from co-workers. All helping professionals should have "a person" on the job to talk to, vent to, and get constructive criticism from—someone they can talk with about the stressors of work.

We, Kaniktra and Andrea, are each other's "person." We work together for an agency that serves individuals who are homeless. We learned early in our careers that our husbands, family members, and friends outside the field do not always understand the stress related to helping others. Therefore, social connectedness with each other and other helping professionals is a vital part of self-care.

Social connectedness with colleagues is one of the important aspects of job satisfaction. It is not all about the work we do; it is also about the relationships with our colleagues. Having a colleague to go to for help, to actively listen when you need to vent, and to share laughs with are all parts of social connectedness. However, to be effective, social connectedness requires authenticity, honesty, and the ability to give and accept constructive criticism. Social connectedness does not involve saying or doing things that do not feel right or to simply please. Not being true to yourself will cause negative energy to build up, which will likely cause dissatisfaction with your role as a helping professional, as well as your role as a colleague. Taking the time to connect with a trusted colleague—whether at your worksite, by phone or email, or for lunch—can bring that spark of joy needed in your day.

"What's on Your Plate?"

All helping professionals should ask themselves this question on a regular basis to keep from becoming overworked, stressed, and overwhelmed. Mathieu (2007) advised: When looking at what is on your plate, "Make a list of all the demands of your time and energy (Work, Family, Home, Health, Volunteering, other)" (p. 2). Do not look at your life with a segmented lens. When thinking about professional and personal obligations, view them as a whole. To better support a balanced life, it is important to consider all responsibilities. In writing this entry, we each looked at our "plates." We realized people are depending on each of us from the time we wake until we go to bed.

We each begin our day with getting our young children up and getting them ready for their day. From there, we begin our workday as helping professionals where people are depending on us to support, guide, nurture, and respond to their needs. After our work day, we transition back into caring for our families. On many of these days, we have other commitments, such as volunteer work, in which we are asked to give of ourselves or our finances or other resources to support other causes. This continuous process can leave us feeling drained mentally, physically, and emotionally. When all of our "selves" are given to others and we do not replenish our energy, we will quickly move into burnout phase. We lose compassion for others because of our own exhaustion.

About a year ago, we worked with a nurse practitioner who did an amazing job. She cared for our clients diligently, was compassionate, and always had a smile on her face. One day, she announced she was leaving to pursue employment elsewhere. When we were able to speak with her personally, she shared about a day when her daughter asked her why she was always so angry. In that moment, she realized she was putting 110% into her work, and when she went home, she had nothing left to give. This story is so true for most helping professionals. Self-care is essential to support our overall wellness. It permeates all areas of our lives.

Time to Care...for Ourselves

Think about a flight you have taken. The flight attendant gave the safety presentation and instructed you to put on your oxygen mask before assisting others. You must take care of yourself before you can care for others. This message is applicable to social work and other helping professions to prevent burnout and increase job satisfaction. What is your "oxygen mask"? What are things you do to take care of yourself, to take a break?

Kaniktra has a colorful handout posted above her desk. The handout is titled "50 Ways to Take a Break" (Oregon State University, n.d.). It provides simple ways to implement self-care and serves as a daily reminder. It includes suggestions such as: let out a sigh, walk outside, color with crayons. This handout is not exhaustive, however. One day, I (Kaniktra) was taking a mini-break at my desk, bouncing a small ball off the wall. I realized that this simple, fun activity gave me a boost of energy. So, I added "bounce a ball against the wall" to the list—and changed the title to "51." Another colleague blows bubbles to relax, and another uses a chime to practice brief breathing exercises.

Add some elements to your workspace that you can readily use for small breaks. Balls, bubbles, or bells: Design your own list of ways to take mini-breaks. Self-care should not be cookie cutter; it should be individualized. (See *Individualized* entry.) When thinking of self-care, create a plan that is tailored to you.

Have an Emergency Plan

Also, we suggest creating an emergency self-care plan and keeping it in plain sight, somewhere you regularly look (e.g., on your desk and/or in your wallet). An emergency self-care plan is necessary because it can be hard to think of what to do for yourself when you are in extremely stressful situations. Therefore, have a plan in place. An emergency self-care plan should include several options you can consider when you feel overwhelmed, a list of people you can talk to, and positive things you can say to yourself. The emergency self-care plan is most effective the better you know yourself and how stress affects you.

For example, I (Kaniktra) have the following items on my emergency self-care plan: listen to music, do a puzzle, talk to my mother and/or mother-in-law, and say to myself "relax" or "accept what you cannot change." I carry this plan, the size of a credit card, in my wallet, along with a puzzle book and earbuds. For me, constant noise and interruptions lead to the inability to focus and increase in irritability, which are a couple of my stress warning signs. In these instances, I put in my earbuds and listen to music. Listening to music brings a sense of tranquility and allows me to refocus.

For Andrea, hunger leads me to feel anxious and stressed. So I keep healthy snacks on hand. so I am physically able to take care of myself. Knowing the stress warning signs you usually experience will give you the opportunity to deal with a stressful situation before the situation worsens and/or your self-care is totally compromised. Having an emergency plan in place will give you a ready resource!

Job satisfaction is not only about the almighty dollar. Being a helping professional is an investment of time, emotions, and energy. The work we do can be very demanding and stressful. It can also bring meaning and joy. Being a helping professional is a labor of love and care for others, but remember, we must love and care for ourselves, as well.

Reflection/Discussion

1. What self-care strategies do you incorporate to improve job satisfaction? How do you find and promote joy in your work?
2. Do you have a person on the job (or in your professional network) you can talk to about the stresses of work?
3. What is on your plate? What could you put on your list of 51 things to do to take a break?
4. What is your emergency "oxygen mask"? Consider designing a personalized, emergency self-care card. What will you include? Where will you keep the card?

Selected Resources

Mathieu, F. (2007, March). *Transforming compassion fatigue into compassion satisfaction: Top 12 self-care tips for helpers.* Retrieved from *http://www.compassionfatigue.org/pages/Top12SelfCareTips.pdf*

Oregon State University. (n.d.). *50 ways to take a break.* Retrieved from *http://success.oregonstate.edu/files/Learning-Corner/Tools/50_ways_to_take_a_break.pdf*

Society for Human Resources Management. (2014, May). *Employee satisfaction and engagement.* Retrieved from *https://www.shrm.org/research/surveyfindings/articles/pages/2012 employeejobsatisfaction.aspx*

Kaizen Method:
Small Changes = Significant Effects
Erlene Grise-Owens

Complete this statement: If at first you don't succeed, _____. Most of us spout the old adage: "Try, Try Again!" But, for self-care purposes, I have found that adage to be largely ineffective and counterproductive. Instead, I suggest completing the statement: If at first you don't succeed...REDEFINE SUCCESS! In this entry, I share how to redefine success, using small and SMART steps.

Redefine Success: Small Steps

Redefining success involves using practical strategies, such as POP—partialize, organize, and prioritize (Grise-Owens, 2013). Likewise, redefining success involves taking small steps, rather than expecting big leaps. Mandel (2005) applies the Japanese management approach of *Kaizen* to stress management. This approach focuses on gradual, continuous improvement. Mandel notes that *kai* means "change" and *zen* means "to become good" (p. 46). She describes this process-oriented approach as making "conscious effort to take small, patient steps" (p. 46), rather than only focusing on dramatic change.

Here is an example of a small change I made early in my growth process of self-care. I started putting self-care commitments on my calendar. Well, the first small change I made was actually using a calendar/planning system. Over decades of giving attention to self-care as part of professional practice, I attest that small changes and redefining success has had significant impact.

First Step to Success: SMART Ways

When working with students/practitioners on their self-care plans, I find that people usually struggle with this "success" trap. For example, "Kassandra" set a goal to walk three times weekly for 20 minutes. For me, that goal would be SMART—because I have been an avid walker for many years and have worked to incorporate this practice into my lifestyle. (In contrast, my colleague's self-care plan of doing aerobics classes five times per week, along with a standard weight-lifting regimen, would be a set-up for total failure for me!) In her accountability reports, however, Kassandra noted that she was unable to achieve "success" with that goal. She was discouraged by her "lack of success."

I invited her to re-define success. I asked: *What is the smallest step/change you can make toward the goal of exercising more?* I made the following Kaizen-type suggestions to spur ideas: (a) take the stairs three times a day, (b) walk three times a week for 10 minutes, (c) make this activity a family outing or commit with a walking partner. En-lightened (i.e., lightened up!) by this insight, Kassandra revised her self-care plan to take her daughter to a nearby park for an hour on a weekly basis. Also, she started taking the two flights of stairs at work. These small changes made for success, which engendered positive energy for ongoing attention to self-care.

A friend, Jenn, who is a fitness coach, says, "If you only make one change: Drink Water!" She goes on to explain that drinking adequate water will positively affect sleep, energy level, digestion, and many other aspects of health and wellness. In her work with clients, Jenn has learned that this small change of drinking more water usually spills over into other areas of life. Feeling more rested and energetic, people are more likely to exercise, focus, and so forth.

Change Your Thinking: Change Your Stress-Success

As part of my commitment to the profession, in addition to teaching self-care in social work courses, colleagues and I offer self-care "well-shops" for community agencies. I emphasize two key complementary ways to change our thinking: "Not everybody's going to like you," and "You're not that important." I joke that I want all of us to get tee shirts (or maybe tattoos!) with these messages. In good humor and humility, I share about my ongoing "recovery" from the addictions of "being liked" and "being important."

Wayne Oates, in 1971, coined the term "workaholic." Using his pastoral counselor context, Oates observed that even the Creator of everything "rested on the Sabbath" (p. 38). He elaborated that this example illustrates how so many fall into the workaholism trap.

All of us in the helping professions deal with these dynamics of workaholism, especially "being important" and "being liked." In preparing for a self-care "well-shop" at a local agency, I asked the participants to email me ahead of time about their successes, struggles, and strategies related to self-care. "Abraham," one of the administrators, asked: "How can I let my staff know that I need to close my door sometimes so that I can get some stuff done?" Another person, "Brianna," asked, "My supervisor sends emails at all times of the night. How can I deal with that?"

In both of these instances, the key to their concern did not have a magic answer. Practically, Abraham simply needed to start closing his door and having sequestered time for paperwork. Brianna needed to know her own boundaries and not respond to emails. (To clarify, she was not expected to be on call.) In these instances—like so many—these solutions would likely cause some discomfort initially. Much of this discomfort is around "being liked" at all times and feeling so important that one must be constantly available. These dynamics take many forms.

But the change in thinking begins with the awareness. I encouraged Abraham to consider what would happen if he explained in the next staff meeting that he was going to enact a sequestered time for paperwork—and encourage others to do so, as well. I brainstormed with Brianna that because her supervisor sent emails at all hours did not mean that she needed to respond at all hours. Sometimes we get so bogged down in our "being liked" and "being important" that we neglect just "being human." These examples illustrate how we can begin to change our thinking and our behaviors.

Perhaps, the above discussion sounds contradictory to the message of this *Handbook*. That is, you are important enough to commit to self-care. Perhaps this analogy will help clarify. When feeling compelled to do more or feeling over-responsible, I remind myself that the change process is like a chain. I am NOT the chain! Rather, I am a link in the chain, which has many other parts—some of which I will never know. This perspective fits with the overall perspective of this entry: Think small, in order to bring significant change. Like Gandhi, be the *change,* but do not take on the responsibility for the entire *chain!*

Self-care is an ongoing journey, which begins with small steps. Take small, SMART steps on the journey of life-long wellness.

Reflection/Discussion

1. What are some self-care goals in which you are being "unsuccessful"? How might you redefine success? What is the smallest change you could make?
2. What are the challenges and benefits you see in using the Kaizen method?
3. Think about organizational wellness and the Kaizen method. What small changes could the agency, your team, or even an accountability group make to change the culture?

Selected Resources

Grise-Owens, E. (2013). Traveling toward a social work degree—Ten road-tested trip-tips. In L. M. Grobman & K. Zgoda (eds.) *The new social worker magazine's back-to-school guide for social work students.* Harrisburg, PA: White Hat Communications.

Mandel, D. (2005, November/December). Small steps, giant gains in self-care. *Social Work Today, 5*(6), 44-47.

Oates, W. E. (1971). *Confessions of a workaholic: The facts about work addiction.* Nashville, TN: Abingdon.

Lifestyle: Self-Care is a Lifestyle, Not an Emergency Response
Derek J. Stephens

In March 2009, I finally made it home from a long, life-changing combat tour in Afghanistan. My journey to a career in social work is driven by the military mindset of "the true meaning of pals." Leaving a comrade (pal) behind is incomprehensible; this ideal fuels my passion to work with the veteran population, including family members.

Likewise, the military mindset focuses heavily on the mission. The mission is always first! Major facets of preparation include knowing what the mission is and having contingencies, in case the mission does not go as initially planned.

Know the Mission and Don't Leave Yourself Behind

The social work field has similarities. Our profession is very mission oriented, with an emphasis on client well-being. Working in the field is challenging and daunting at times. It is easy to become fixated on our clients' problems. To some degree, we go above and beyond the call of duty to "not leave them behind." In doing so, we can lose ourselves along the way. Many of us share the passion to help, aid, and assist our clients. The thought of their suffering tears us up inside. However, we can fixate so much on others that we forget about our own well-being. Then, before we know it, we are the ones "left behind." Tunnel vision leads to our own demise.

Recently, I read *Taking Care of Business and a Few Other Things Along the Way.* In this brief article, Laferriere (2014) noted the importance of not waiting until at the verge of burnout to start self-care. Laferriere clarified that self-care should be done simply to enjoy life more. Furthermore, Laferriere emphasized that we need to keep self-care simple!

I have learned that self-care has to be a lifestyle, not an emergency response. We cannot wait until we "stroke out" from stress and end up in the emergency room from personal neglect or find ourselves in an ethically compromised situation. Further, self-care has to be a way of life in order to strengthen our abilities to be in the moment, thus enhancing the ability to build therapeutic alliances and provide service delivery. This lifestyle of self-care decreases burnout and compassion fatigue.

Contingency Plans and Living Life

Self-care does not have to be complicated, but it does need to be multi-faceted and comprehensive. Self-care simply starts by increasing awareness and developing a SMART plan. However, there is no such thing as a perfect plan. We have to be flexible. Things come up, sessions go over, people get sick, and appointments change: Life! Therefore, I recommend to always have a contingency plan, when an event occurs that takes you off your plan. Remember, it does not have to be complicated. It can be as simple as stopping to breathe. I suggest taking a time-out daily to critically reflect. During this time of mindfulness (being in the present moment), notice yourself. Notice what is consuming your thoughts. If you are finding it difficult to think of anything other than "fixing" clients, you may be experiencing tunnel vision. We are taught to set clear and professional boundaries with clients and colleagues. Should we not do the same with ourselves?

Self-care is living life. This philosophy became crucial to my well-being and professional health when I began a graduate program with a 6-hour commute every other weekend, while working a full-time job, doing a practicum…and welcoming our fourth child to our family. I wanted to savor all these experiences. I could not add "self-care" activities to my full plate!

Instead, I focused on being present to my life. Breathing, listening to music, enjoying a cup of coffee, sharing time with family and friends, or going for a walk are part of a self-care lifestyle. Self-care can be throwing a baseball with your kids, enjoying the quietness during your commute to and from work, or going out on a date with your sweetheart.

Self-care is simply enjoying life by doing something you find enjoyable—and focusing on the joy in all you do.

Self-care is also not just something you do after work. It is part of the lifestyle *during* work. Being a helping professional is hectic at times for all of us. We are loaded to the fullest with work, but we can still do self-care without over-complicating it. The most important advice I have adapted is to incorporate self-care into my LIFE. It is not work and *then* life; instead, it is a life balance that includes work. (See *Balance* entry.) This *Handbook* gives countless ideas to incorporate. Don't wait for an emergency to "do" self-care. Make it a lifestyle. Let's enjoy life, savor the moment, and continue to be all that we can be as professionals—and human beings.

Reflection/Discussion

1. What is your mission?
2. What are some healthy ways to decrease tunnel vision?
3. What are some ways to keep from leaving yourself and loved ones behind?
4. How can you make self-care a lifestyle? What does your "contingency plan" include?

Selected Resource

Laferriere, M. (2014). Taking care of business and a few other things along the way. *The New Social Worker.* Retrieved from *http://www.socialworker.com/feature-articles/practice/ taking-care-of-business-and-a-few-other-things-along-the-way/*

Mindfulness
Kathy Lay

Mindfulness is one of the simplest, yet hardest, ways to engage in self-care. It is simple, because it can be done anywhere at any time. It is hard, because it is counter to the multi-tasking, distracted mindset of the dominant Western culture. However, I have found that the difficulty is well worth the effort, and the simplicity has powerful effects.

Mindfulness is defined as being in the present moment non-judgmentally (Siegel, 2007). It does not mean critiquing the present moment, as in: it is a beautiful sunny day, or it is too hot outside, and so forth. It simply means being in this moment as it is with the breath, mind, body, and surroundings, as it is. Certainly, we make observations about our discomfort, and many discomforts call for adaptation, but without judgment.

Not Noticing: Mindlessness

We all understand what it means to have the habit of being in a mindless state. Take, for example, the drive to work. We often take the same route. Our brain memorizes it, forms a habit, and we arrive with little memory of any nuances of the drive. We may not notice the woman who stands at the bus stop on a particular corner. We may not even notice the bus stop. We are preoccupied. Perhaps we are planning our day or rehearsing a morning meeting. Once at work, we grab a coffee, without thought to who made it or who brought the pastries. Sitting down in the meeting, we greet our co-workers and launch the agenda, not noticing that one of our co-workers is struggling to sit in a chair without pain. You get the picture.

We have all participated to some degree or another in not noticing—being mindless. A few years ago, a friend recounted to me that, on his vacation, he noticed he was enjoying himself. Then, he wondered if he would enjoy his next vacation as much as this one. He told me, "I knew I was in trouble with that kind of thinking." Like my friend, I knew I spent a lot of my life on the fast track, living in the next moment to the next week, month, and year. This way of operating went beyond planning. It was about NOT being present.

Suffering: Opening the Door to Mindfulness

As a social worker, I know that mindfulness has gained momentum in clinical practice. For example, mindfulness was the thematic topic in the January/February 2015 issue of the popular professional magazine, *Psychotherapy Networker.* Featuring several articles on mindfulness, the magazine cover declared, "Mindfulness goes viral...." Books such as *The Zen of Helping* and *Mindfulness and Social Work* inform professional practice. Beck (2016) wrote "Mindfulness: 10 Lessons in Self-Care for Social Workers" in the Winter 2016 issue of *The New Social Worker.*

Yet, like many others, I came to mindfulness through suffering intense personal pain. This personal introduction to mindfulness came in 2007 when I became interested in how the brain responds to pain. While getting dressed one morning, I injured my back. Pain was immediate. I had a busy day ahead and ignored the stinging lower back pain. I dismissed the persistent pain and proceeded to go about my hectic day and week. The weekend arrived, and I was scheduled to do a 30-mile bike ride with the local bike club. My spouse asked me to consider resting and skipping the ride, because of my pain. I refused. The pain heightened throughout the ride. As I rolled to the finish, the pain radiated up my right leg. Needless to say, I found myself in the emergency room later that evening. The rehabilitation process was tedious and took me through several care providers. Relief came from a physical therapist teaching me three simple exercises and recommending yoga.

Then, spring break came and I had enough relief from my back pain to go on a much-needed trip to the beach. Supplied with my new yoga book, mat, and Siegel's (2007) *The Mindful Brain,* I set out to make some changes. I was up early one morning by the pool with my yoga mat and how-to-book, making my best effort to practice yoga. A woman, enjoying the sunshine, asked, "Would you mind if I give you a few pointers on your postures? I am a yoga instructor and would be glad to help." "Please," I answered. I became curious about the connection between yoga, meditation, mindfulness, and pain relief. My back improved. Yoga and my curiosity waxed and waned.

Then, the cosmos handed me a critical reminder. In the spring of 2009, I began to notice that I seemed to have a lot of pain a lot of the time. In a short span, I was diagnosed with rheumatoid arthritis and, subsequently, fibromyalgia. This pronouncement was a low blow.

Once again, I returned to thoughts of pain management. I enrolled in a Mindfulness-Based Stress Reduction (MBSR) course. MBSR was developed by Jon Kabat-Zinn (2013) for individuals to help manage stress, pain, and illness. Today, MBSR courses are available in most metropolitan cities and communities, often affiliated with medical centers and universities. As a critical pragmatist, I continued to research mindfulness and its effects on the brain. I learned about the connections between neurology (mind), biology (body), and spirituality (spirit)—which were "known" by the ancients (e.g., Hanson & Mendius, 2009).

My personal suffering opened the door to the practice of mindfulness. Currently, I practice daily meditation, continue to practice yoga, and practice mindfulness as a way of being in the world. I have incorporated these practices into my professional social work roles as a professor and therapist. The key word is practice. A family member asked me if mindfulness and meditation took away my pain. I responded, "No. It has changed my relationship to pain." Like any relationship, a more positive relationship with pain requires consistent practices.

Mindfulness, Meditation, and Self-Compassion: Noticing and Being

Mindfulness practice is *a way of being in the present moment.* "We approach our here-and-now experience with curiosity, openness, acceptance, and love (COAL)" (Siegel, 2007, p. 15). A formal meditation practice is a way to bring a repeated discipline to the mind, body, and spirit. This discipline is a way of bringing the intention of living mindfully into each day. Loving-kindness is critical to mindfulness practice. This practice means to be compassionate toward self, others, and adopting kindness as a way of being. Don't be fooled by self-critical degrading messages in an effort to motivate toward improved behaviors. No evidence supports that degradation and shaming, as ways of being in the world, makes for anything other than unnecessary suffering.

We all desire to be happy and, likewise, deserve happiness. As living, breathing, human beings, we will experience suffering. We cannot escape this fate, although our culture encourages a variety of ways to escape, many of which lead to more suffering. Compassion is the antidote for suffering—not to escape, but to live with our human condition.

Compassion means noticing our own suffering and the suffering of others without judgment. According to Neff (2011), "We can't be moved by our own pain if we don't even acknowledge that it exists in the first place" (p. 10). Acknowledging our own pain affords us an opportunity to see the pain and suffering in others. The person who trailed the bumper of my car and then whipped around at high speed giving me a dirty look is a fellow human being, suffering. The person who offended you last week is a fellow human being, suffering. We do not know their stories. Noticing with compassion and curiosity brings the possibility to be open to experiences with our common planet dwellers and respond with loving-kindness.

Mindfulness: It is a practice. It is not a competition—even with oneself. It is a practice.

As MBSR teacher Kathleen Beck-Coon (personal communication, n.d.) says, "It's just like this right now."

Reflection/Discussion

1. Take a moment to connect with your breath. Set an intention to be with your breath for three to five minutes—breathing naturally. Thoughts will come. Treat them non-judgmentally, as if they were clouds floating

by. Reflect on your observations of self in this experience, without judgment.
2.   Set an intention to explore mindfulness practices for the next thirty days and discuss what you have learned with an interested colleague. Discuss how these ways of being may influence your professional practice.

Selected Resources

Beck, D. L. (2016). Mindfulness: 10 lessons in self-care for social workers. *The New Social Worker, 23*(1), 9-11.

Bein, A. W. (2008). *The Zen of helping.* Hoboken, NJ: John Wiley & Sons.

Hanson, R. (with Mendius, R.) (2009). *The practical neuroscience of Buddha's brain: Happiness, love, and wisdom.* Oakland, CA: New Harbinger Publications.

Hick, S. F. (2009). *Mindfulness and social work.* Chicago, IL: Lyceum.

Kabat-Zinn, J. (2013). *Full catastrophe living: Using the wisdom of your body and mind to face stress, pain, and illness.* (Revised Edition). New York, NY: Bantam Books.

Neff, K. (2011). *Self-compassion: The proven power of being kind to yourself.* New York, NY: William Morrow, A Division of Harper Collins.

Siegel, D. J. (2007). *The mindful brain: Reflection and attunement in the cultivation of well-being.* New York, NY: W.W. Norton & Company.

Nature
Mindy Eaves

The philosopher Aristotle proclaimed, "…in all things of nature, there is something marvelous." Nature is like a cool cleansing rain, washing away the troubles laid before me. As a helping professional, I delve deeply into others' problems, empathize with their feelings, and discuss problem-solving strategies. Incorporating nature into my self-care plan was essential to ward off the hazards, such as burnout, of being a helping professional.

"Bogged Down?" Create a Bog Garden

In nature, I find rejuvenation, peace, and balance. Although I live in an urban area, working in my bog garden is quiet and peaceful. It serves as a gentle reminder of how nature, like people, is resilient. Regardless of the harsh environment, nature always finds a way to replenish.

Some years ago, an area of my home landscape was overly shady, very wet, and seemingly hopeless for any growth. At the same time, I was experiencing tremendous workplace stress and desperately needed new ways to effectively manage stress. Like my home landscape, I felt stymied in my professional growth.

I read that taking a walk outside was a great way to "bust a bad mood" (Best Ways to Bust…, 2011). I began taking walks around my office building. While walking under trees and around yard benches, the pathways were natural and minimally disturbed the environment. The walks cleared my mind, boosted energy, and sparked ideas. Research shows that a connection to nature reduces stress and cultivates a sense of meaning and purpose (e.g., Ulrich et al., 1991).

Eventually, I began taking "nature walks" with my family at home, and we fell in love with nature. This feeling of connection to nature helped me experience the restorative power of nature and sparked an idea to appreciate the environment, even what seemed beyond repair. These nature walks evolved to creating a bog garden at home. Boggy soil is soft, watery and typically referred to as a trouble spot where very few plants, trees, and so forth can grow. The entire eastern side of my home was comprised of boggy soil. I transformed this "hopeless" area of my home into a serene, rejuvenating place that provides me peace.

Feeling bogged down, I simply decided to create a bog garden. A collection of perennials, shrubs, and trees that thrive under consistently moist and shady conditions, a bog garden often has water features such as a pond or fountain. I walk through my garden several times each week. I reserve heavy-duty work, such as digging and lifting in the garden, for days when I experience increased work stress. The heavy-duty work serves as a therapeutic output of energy and a healthy way to relieve stress (Wolf, Krueger, & Rozance, 2014).

Like my discovery of bog gardening, I stumbled into the Louisville Loop when exploring ways to expand my self-care options. The city has several green spaces connected by scenic pathways, referred to as the Louisville Loop. The pathway stretches around the cityscape through hilly parks and along the river. In spring, aromatic honeysuckle shrubs scent and burgundy Japanese maples accent the pathway—serving as a natural meditative space. Japanese culture emphasizes the healing power of nature. Shinrin-yoku ("forest bathing") is a concept that means walking through the woods to experience nature's restorative power (Hutchinson, 2013). Benefits of forest bathing include minimal noise pollution, clean air, and immune-boosting mist from plants.

At work, my day is filled with meetings and tasks, with minimal down time and even less for processing. The nature pathway provides a space with few distractions and quiet time, leaving me alone with only my thoughts. Likewise, in my bog garden, I become immersed in the solitude and peace of nature. Nature is quiet and simple. I share bell hooks' (2000) sentiment that the key is to live life simply. In these quiet times, in the bog garden and on the nature path, I find clear thoughts and creative ideas.

Bring Nature Into Your Workday

Ansel Adams, who believed nature provided endless prospects of "magic and wonder," is known for his photography of natural landscapes. I incorporated similar photos of nature and live plants into my office decor to provide a relaxing atmosphere. Infusing nature into my workspace has a rejuvenating effect. It allows me time to re-center before meeting with the next client or going to that long meeting. Researchers found that people who had nature contact experienced "significantly lower stress levels and health complaints than those with less natural elements in their workspace" (Largo-Wight, 2013). Nature scenes as a screensaver, desk fountains, Zen gardens, plants, or pictures capturing nature are ways to bring nature into the workspace.

Elements of nature in your office can engage all your senses. For instance, having nature sounds playing as a background while working can soothe the stress. A colleague uses essential oils as a part of her self-care plan. She uses natural scents, such as lavender and peppermint, to infuse her office space. The subtle scents in her office are olfactory reminders of the healing powers of nature.

As a "natural" de-stressor, nature helps maintain a healthy balance for helping professionals. Dedicating time in nature—whether working in a garden, traveling through scenic pathways, or infusing nature into your work surroundings—is a natural step toward developing a well-rounded self-care plan.

Reflection/Discussion

1. Think about your work surroundings and nature. What are some ways to infuse nature into your workspace?
2. Think about the location of your office. Is there a park, waterway, or other natural setting you can visit during breaks?
3. A bog garden was just what I needed when I was feeling "bogged down" in my professional life. Where is a natural setting or activity that can help you feel rejuvenated and replenished?

Selected Resources

Adams, A. (1961, January 1). *Commencement address at Occidental College.* Lecture conducted from Remsen Bird Hillside Theater, Berkeley, California.

Best ways to bust a bad mood. (2011, October 3). Retrieved from *http://theemployeeassistanceprogram.com/wp/2011/10/03/best-ways-to-bust-a-bad-mood/*

hooks, b. (2000). *All about love: New visions.* New York, NY: William Morrow.

Hutchinson, A. (2013, March). Why is walking in the woods so good for you? *The Globe and Mail.* Retrieved from *http://www.theglobeandmail.com/life/health-and-fitness/fitness/why-is-walking-in-the-woods-so-good-for-you/article4209703/*

Largo-Wight, E. (2013, December). *The nature prescription: Bring nature inside your home and office.* Retrieved from: *http://fitnesscenter.bobgear.com/fitnesscenter/author/erin-largowight/*

Ulrich, R., Simons, R., Losito, B., Fiorito, E., Miles, M., & Zelson, M. (1991). Stress recovery during exposure to natural and urban environments. *Journal of Environmental Psychology, 201-230.*

Why nature is therapeutic. (n.d.). Retrieved July 1, 2015, from *http://www.crchealth.com/find-a-treatment-center/struggling-youth-programs/help/nature-is-therapeutic/*

Wolf, K., Krueger, S., & Rozance, M. (2014). Stress, wellness & physiology—a literature review. In *Green Cities: Good Health.* Retrieved from *http://www.greenhealth.washington.edu*

Organizational Wellness
Ellen Kelley

This *Handbook* is primarily about how to practice self-care as an individual practitioner. After decades in the field, I have learned the importance of this individual attention and the impact it can have. I have also learned that, regardless of the level within the organizational hierarchy, everyone working in the human services field is subject to stress and burnout. And, as an administrator and now director of training for my agency, I know that individual self-care (person) and organizational wellness (place) intersect.

Organizational Leadership's Role in Fostering Organizational Wellness

The agency culture has significant impact on employees (Lotmore, 2014). Giving attention to organizational wellness is crucial. Organizations committed to wellness will actively promote employee health and well-being, as well as organizational performance and productivity.

Cox and Steiner (2013) identify the following aspects of organizations that foster wellness:

- employee involvement;
- life balance;
- employee growth and development;
- health and safety; and
- employee recognition.

Organizational leaders, such as administrators and supervisors, should continuously strive to strengthen these. This can be achieved through attention to policies, such as vacation and paid leave and training/professional development opportunities. Also, these aspects can be seen in processes, such as level of staff input in changes. Finally, these wellness aspects can be seen in the organization's culture and climate. Examples include formal and informal mechanisms for protections against discrimination and harassment, as well as flexibility and autonomy in work patterns.

For management, reducing stress at all levels in the organization can lead to improved employee retention, increased productivity, and fewer workplace accidents (Cox & Steiner, 2013). And for employees, reducing or learning to cope with the stresses of an ill-functioning or even toxic organization can improve your digestive process, save your marriage, or even save your life (Clarke & Cooper, 2004). Unfortunately, it is too easy for management to blame stress problems on an employee's nature, age, mental health history, or other individual factors. Likewise, employees can find fault with managerial style, lack of resources, or other organizational factors. But stress problems lie "neither in the person or the place but the relationship between the two" (Clarke & Cooper, p. 7).

Relating to the Organization: Reduce Stressors, Improve Reactions, Minimize Consequences

In their book, *Managing the Risk of Workplace Stress,* Clarke and Cooper (2004) describe a framework for stress intervention. The primary (preventative) step is to reduce the number or intensity of stressors. They suggest considering ways to do a job redesign. Is one part of your job particularly stressful? Consider how you might reduce that stress. Perhaps you need more training, a better computer, or a quieter place to work. Is the most stressful part of your job something someone else really enjoys doing? Think of a trade or getting the help of a co-worker. For instance, a colleague shared with me how she and a group of staff discussed the problems they were having with completing timely documentation. They brainstormed and identified several strategies to streamline the paperwork process—including changing some of the forms. Also, they established a sequestered hour daily for documentation (door closed, no interruptions). These employees came up with this plan and presented it to their supervisor; that is, they did not wait for the organization to make changes. (See *Workspace* entry.)

In another example, Miller, Hubble, and Mathieu (2015) describe how one clinical agency began tracking quality of work and outcomes on a monthly basis. They began discharging or referring clients (oftentimes to therapists within the same agency) who were not making progress toward outcomes. Miller, Hubble, and Mathieu contended that staff burnout is most directly related to staff experiences of feeling compelled to keep working with client situations that show little progress, i.e., ineffective care. The management of this agency promoted a cultural shift: "It wasn't considered a problem when the measures showed, despite everyone's best efforts, that the therapy wasn't working" (p. 42). This shift enhanced choice and effectiveness and promoted other steps, such as staff having flexible schedules. Notably, the agency has experienced improved client outcomes and satisfaction, overall, as well as reduced staff turnover and sick days.

Clarke and Cooper's (2004) secondary (preventative/reactive) step is to improve your reactions to the stressors you are not able to remove. This step includes various forms of stress management and wellness training. Other entries in this *Handbook* provide an excellent array of strategies. If stress is connected to communication issues in your workplace, how can you improve the information sharing between colleagues? I was working in a job where everyone was out of the office for most of the day. By changing the one hour, one-day-a-week staff meeting to half-hour meetings two days a week, the communication among staff improved and the stress levels were reduced. Some teams at that agency had a 15-minute meeting every morning. Sharing information every morning gave employees a greater sense of control and reduced their anxiety.

The third (tertiary) step involves minimizing the damaging consequences of stress by focusing on the treatment of stress-related problems once they occur. Again, this *Handbook* draws attention to some of these steps. In general, seek medical and/or health services regularly, exercise, improve your nutrition, and seek support from a counselor. Many agencies provide free short-term counseling through an employee assistance plan (EAP). Managers need to be supportive of the use of the EAP. If an EAP is not available, counseling could be covered by your health insurance or available through a community agency or religious organization.

Consider Goodness of Fit Between You and an Organization

If these three steps don't result in helpful reduction in your stress level, you may need to find a new position with a more appropriate supervisor or in a healthier environment. When looking for a new job, our thoughts are usually consumed with making a favorable impression on the interviewer. But interview skills should include assessing how you will function in the organization.

Consider the goodness of fit between you and the organization. *(Goodness of fit* is a systems term that refers to the interaction between persons and environment.) Consider the organizational vision, mission, values, diversity, and culture (Cox & Steiner, 2013). For example, assess whether the employees are treated fairly. Do colleagues share information and support each other (Clarke, 2004)? Ask questions, such as: How will this organization support stress management? Are the pay and benefits adequate? Nothing is more stressful than worrying about how your bills will be paid. Notably, this goodness of fit analysis is helpful in the process of deciding whether to stay at an organization or leave.

In assessing a potential new supervisor or organization, look for evidence of:

- instrumental support (help of a practical nature that is important to you);
- emotional support (interest in and sympathy for employees' difficulties);
- informational support (information is power—is it shared or hoarded?); and
- appraisal support or feedback about the job functioning (Clarke & Cooper, 2004, p. 24).

You also need to determine what support is most important to you. One of my favorite jobs was at an agency where the budget was so tight that we had to buy our own pens, Post-it notes, and toilet paper. But, for me, the emotional and appraisal support made up for what was lacking in the instrumental support.

At another agency, one supervisor did not value appraisal and emotional support (e.g., this supervisor insisted that we not share anything of a personal nature at work). So, when budgets tightened and a memo went out that company supplied tissues were only to be used by paying clients, it was the last straw. Employees quit en masse. Once I had a job where I wasn't sure who my supervisor was—the government agency where my office was housed, the university that had obtained the grant to pay my salary, or the volunteer committee that oversaw my work product. I got minimal emotional or appraisal support. When I resigned, I was shocked with the positive feedback I finally received about my performance.

Deciding to change jobs can be scary. And looking for a new job can be stressful itself. But it is less stressful to look for employment when you are still employed. Don't wait until workplace anxiety causes illness or reduced productivity and you are forced to look for other employment.

Reinhold (1996) gives a strategy I have found helpful for finding the courage to change jobs. First, identify 10 people you know who were able to escape unhealthy or toxic situations. Talk with them about how they did it. Second, visualize a positive work environment and how you can get there. Third, writing or journaling can be valuable, because it moves the subconscious to where you can analyze rationally. The fourth step, brainwalking, is like brainstorming, in which you create inspired solutions to your employment problems. And, lastly, seeking out career counselors and other forms of short-term therapy can be a good support in getting the courage to change your life.

Reflection/Discussion

1. Reflect on the aspects identified in organizational wellness. How does your organization rate? How might you celebrate success and/or encourage improvement in these aspects?
2. What can you do to reduce the intensity of workplace stress? Improve your reactions to stressors you are not able to remove or reduce? Minimize the consequences of stress?
3. Consider the goodness of fit between you and your current organization. Consider the factors that might result in your seeking another job and strategies for that search.

Selected Resources

Clarke, S., & Cooper, C. (2004). *Managing the risk of workplace stress.* New York, NY: Routledge.

Cox, K., & Steiner, S. (2013). *Self-care in social work: A guide for practitioners, supervisors, and administrators.* Washington, DC: NASW Press.

Lotmore, A. (2014). The importance of agency culture and balanced boundaries. *The New Social Worker, 21*(4), 8-9.

Miller, S., Hubble, M., & Mathieu, F. (2015). Burnout reconsidered. *Psychotherapy Networker, 39(3), 18-23, 42-43.*

Reinhold, B. B. (1996). *Toxic work: How to overcome stress, overload, and burnout and revitalize your career.* New York, NY: Dutton.

Professional Development:
Self-Care Beyond the Spa
Nicole George

References to self-care usually engender visions of activities such as vacations and spa visits. Professional development is not a conventional idea for self-care, as it is not associated with oceanfront views or massages. Investment in professional development involves expending energy and time and perhaps even being willing to embrace discomfort. In essence, professional development is often seen as an extension of work—and, as such, not viewed as an antidote to burnout.

Yet, growing evidence suggests that learning new skills, expanding knowledge, and diversifying areas of interest can reduce stress and burnout. For example, Orlinsky and Ronnestad (2005) did a comprehensive study with more than 10,000 psychotherapists in over a dozen countries. They identified professional development as a key motivator in sustaining practitioners, as well as a significant protective factor against burnout. Similarly, Miller, Hubble, and Mathieu (2015) found that practitioners who report professional satisfaction and have productive career performance invest significant time in professional development activities. In other words, a key to sustaining our practice is giving intentional attention to more effectively and efficiently engaging in our work.

In this entry, I recount how I have used professional development to battle through burnout and renew my commitment to working in child welfare. As well, I suggest ways that organizations can benefit from and contribute to professional development.

Mentoring and Mobility

NASW (n.d.) defines professional development as, "a self-directed process which requires social workers to assume responsibility for the growth of their own professional knowledge base" (para. 1). Although framed as "self-directed," I've always been incredibly fortunate to have guidance from strong mentors in my professional development. Mentors both within academia and in the workplace are associated with an array of positive outcomes. For example, Gutierrez (2012), reporting on social work students' use of mentors, found that, "students who have had positive mentors are more likely to do well in school, be more productive, have stronger professional skills, be more confident and have larger professional networks" (p.1). Throughout my graduate experience and into my post-graduate career, I was mentored by a school faculty member who taught me that ethical practice meant being accountable to oneself with regard to self-care. My mentor is a model for self-care practice within her professional role in academia, where she continues to demonstrate how the practice of self-care enables one to practice effectively within an imperfect system.

Within the workplace, mentoring can also be a factor in career development (Gutierrez, 2012). Early in my career, I was befriended by a retired child welfare worker who advised me to move throughout the agency and take every opportunity to learn different program areas and develop new skills. This advice proved invaluable. In accepting different positions within the child welfare agency, I've been able to learn new programs and stay challenged in an environment where the suffocating workload doesn't lend itself to accepting additional work. This process required giving deliberate attention to learning other areas of practice and seeking guidance from those who had successfully carved a path in the profession.

Through my experience, I learned that being strategic about when to change positions is essential. According to Maclean (2011), burnout may be accompanied by a lack of motivation. If one isn't proactive in positioning oneself for the next position before burnout sets in, it can be even more difficult to put ideas in motion or devote the mental energy necessary for developing new skills.

Life-Long Learning and Contributing
to the Knowledge Base

An important part of professional development is seeking out opportunities such as trainings, conferences, and continuing education. Licensure is an important way of committing to professional development, because retaining one's license requires ongoing education. In a more involved way, certifications, such as Certification in Drug and Alcohol Counseling or myriad other areas, can also promote professional development and increase marketability.

Scholarship is another way to engage in professional development. The NASW (2008) *Code of Ethics* directs social workers to:

> ...*contribute to the knowledge base of social work and share with colleagues their knowledge related to practice, research, and ethics. Social workers should seek to contribute to the profession's literature and to share their knowledge at professional meetings and conferences. (Section 5.01d)*

I have presented at local, national, and even global conferences. Likewise, I have begun adjunct teaching at my alma mater. This involvement enhances my own professional development and contributes to the profession, while leaving me rejuvenated.

Similarly, I am active in professional organizations, such as my alma mater's MSW alumni organization. This activity extends my networks and offers more opportunities for continuing education. For example, our Alumni leadership offers a book club. Alumni facilitate a discussion on a professional book, and the school provides continuing education credits.

Being proactive in professional development has allowed me to divert attention away from some of the negativity of the day-to-day and, instead, direct energy and focus to something that enriches my practice. Furthermore, it offers me a bigger practice net in which to catch and enhance my marketability. And, finally, it energizes me professionally to be a contributor to our knowledge base.

Organization's Role and Benefits

Using professional development as a means to ward off burnout is not just the business of the individual social worker or other helping professional. I've had excellent mentors and have pursued opportunities for professional development along my professional journey. However, agency policies to promote professional development have been notably absent.

In promoting professional development, agencies have an opportunity to reduce burnout in their workforce and enhance retention, thereby, ensuring higher quality services. The links between job satisfaction and stress have been well documented (e.g., Cox & Steiner, 2013). Maclean (2011) describes the use of job enlargement (i.e., a variety of different types of work within their position) as an opportunity for addressing burnout. An agency's ability to implement policies that encourage staff to learn different programs or practice skills is one example of a low-cost mechanism for reducing burnout. Policies that allocate funds for continuing education opportunities and grant leave time for professional development serve to benefit the agency's workforce and the service population. Providing support for mentoring programs to ensure less seasoned workers have access to knowledge about opportunities beyond their current positions and skills necessary for mobility creates an environment of shared learning, which contributes to the overall health of an organization. (See *Organizational Wellness* entry.)

Professional development as a self-care practice skill is concentrated on the long-term, but also has immediate tangible benefits. It gives the practitioner knowledge, confidence, and control in a professional world where such variables may be scarce. Professional development is one of the most empowering forms of self-care, as it has potential to elevate mind and spirit. It can change how we see ourselves, our work, and our professional environment.

Reflection/Discussion

1. How do you engage in professional development? What might be some ways to enhance professional development as self-care?
2. How might you use mentoring and/or mobility to support your self-care?
3. What do you think of the connection between contributing to the professional knowledge base as a way to (re) energize your career and as a form of self-care? What might be some ways to incorporate this aspect into your career and self-care plan?
4. How does your organization support employee professional development? How might that support be enhanced?

Selected Resources

Cox, K., & Steiner, S. (2013). *Self-care in social work: A guide for practitioners, supervisors, and administrators.* Washington, DC: NASW Press.

Gutierrez, L. M. (2012). Recognizing and valuing our roles as mentors. *Journal of Social Work Education, 48*(1), 1-4.

Maclean, S. (2011). *The social worker pocket guide to stress and burnout.* Mesnes Green, Lichfield, Staffordshire, England: Kirwin Maclean Associates.

Miller, S., Hubble, M., & Mathieu, F. (2015). Burnout reconsidered. *Psychotherapy Networker, 39*(3), 18-23, 42-43.

NASW. (2008). *Code of ethics.* Washington, DC: NASW.

NASW (n.d). *Practice and professional development.* Retrieved from *http://www.naswdc.org/pdev/default.asp*

Orlinsky, D., & Ronnestad, M. H. (2005). *How psychothera-pists develop: A study of therapeutic work and professional growth.* Washington, DC: American Psychological Association.

Quality (Not Necessarily Quantity)
Laura Escobar-Ratliff

Prioritizing and integrating self-care into my life has been like trying to navigate through a labyrinth. Just as I thought I had found the "right" way, I would run into a barrier. More often than not, the barrier I encountered seemed to be "time." When do I fit in time for self-care? What do I have to move or adjust to make time for self-care? It was not that I did not want to make time for self-care. I have become well aware of the importance of self-care and the need to prioritize it. The barrier became what to do about competing priorities. How do I fit in time for work, family, church, child, partner, pet, household chores, exercise, friends, and so on and on and on?

Not How Much; Rather, How Meaningful

Our society focuses on quantity. How much does one work? How much does one exercise? How much time does one spend with her/his child/family? How much time is spent volunteering? How much? How much? How much? I, too, was stuck in how much. Then, I realized, by focusing solely on how much, I had lost sight of how good. What was the quality behind the quantity?

When describing quality, Keeps (2007, Summer) stated that "the one consistent attribute of real quality is its endurance. [When] we recognize quality, we connect to a larger truth, either about ourselves or about human nature" (para. 2). In trying to excel in all aspects of life, including self-care, I had gotten bogged down in *how much* self-care, as contrasted with how *memorable, valuable, truthful,* and *enduring* was my self-care. Recognizing this difference became a freeing experience, because it shifted my thinking in how to execute my self-care.

Rather than focusing on what and how much, I focused on what and how meaningful. How connected was I to my self-care? How mindful was I when engaging in self-care?

How individualized were my self-care activities to the phase of life I was in at that time? What was enduring?

Asking myself these questions allowed me to better integrate my self-care with my daily life, which is a key to successful self-care! Being a social worker, an educator, a mom, a partner, a daughter, a sister, a friend, a pet owner, a home owner, and so on pulled me in multiple directions. I took time to reflect on what I engage in that is memorable, valuable, and creates enduring memories—time with my partner, time with my daughter, time with good friends/colleagues, and fun. Also, I considered which aspects of my work life were most meaningful. Instead of focusing on each aspect of my life as a silo of events, I began to look at it as an integrative puzzle.

Making the Mundane (More) Meaningful

Deliberately integrating self-care into my daily routine to enhance the quality (e.g., endurance and connectivity) has become freeing. Now a mundane task like grocery shopping becomes quality time and a fun activity with my daughter. This honoring of the mundane is part of a wonderful approach that Rechtschaffen (1996) calls "timeshifting." (See *Time* entry.) I am learning how to shift how I view time—and by extension, self-care. Grocery shopping is an example of a mundane activity. In timeshifting, I allot time so that before we shop for our grocery needs, my daughter and I simply stroll up and down the aisles. She loves to point out all the different items she can read and that she finds interesting. After about 30 minutes or so of perusing the aisles, she is ready to settle into the shopping cart and help me find the items on our grocery list. I get extra walking in and 1:1 time with my daughter, as I beam with pride at how much she's learning. I get the shopping done and I get to glow when others tell me how she is so cute and well behaved.

Another example of this mundane approach is addressing physical well-being. Eating healthier and getting more exercise is a family goal. My partner and I serve as accountability partners for one another, supporting one another in our exercise, healthy choices, and the occasional unhealthy splurge. Addressing physical health as a family unit allows us to support, encourage, challenge, and tease one another. Our daily toning exercises have become a pre-dinner family event for everyone.

Similar to these family times, I also considered ways to make the mundane aspects of my work day more meaningful. For example, in my efforts to do *more* through multitasking, I would try to work at home in the evenings, while simultaneously being available to my daughter. One evening, my daughter said, "I thought you were going to be home tonight, Mommy." With awareness that I was not really being present, my partner and I have gotten more intentional about scheduling my office hours, or I go to a nearby coffee shop for sequestered work time. This focused work time allows me to be more fully present *both* to my work *and* in the quality time with my daughter and partner.

I could provide a variety of examples in which self-care has been integrated into my daily life with a focus on quality. It is never a perfect timeshift, but it is a qualitative difference. You can do the same.

Begin by thinking about what are meaningful self-care needs. Then think about integration. How can your self-care be integrated into your daily routine? How does this integration affect your connectivity with loved ones, nature, meaningful work, a higher power, and so forth? How present, how mindful, are you when engaging in your daily life? How individualized is your self-care to the phase of life you are in at this time? Tailoring your self-care to your phase of life will increase your ability to be present to that moment in life. Increased presence/mindfulness will lead to increased connectivity. Increased connectivity results in meaning and endurance.

These elements will enhance the quality of your self-care, as contrasted with the quantity. Then, you may discover that you actually have more time for self-care, because you are engaged in the mundane in meaningful ways.

Reflection/Discussion

1. What activities can you engage in that will create enduring memories?
2. How can self-care strategies be integrated into mundane activities of your daily living?
3. How can you incorporate loved ones in your self-care goals?

Selected Resources

Keeps, D. (2007, Summer). What is quality? *O Magazine.* Retrieved from *http://www.oprah.com/oathome/O-at-Home-Summer-2007-Ask-Yourself-What-Is Quality*

Rechtschaffen, S. (1996). *Time-shifting—Creating more time to enjoy your life.* New York, NY: Doubleday.

Relationships: Cultivating Your Garden
Wade Drury

Managing stress and avoiding burnout is not something we do on our own. We need others. Good relationships are key in our self-care. We must cultivate relationships with people who provide the kind of emotional and professional support we need. We should engage in relationships with people who genuinely listen to us and give critical feedback that aims to build us up and promote growth. However, not all relationships encourage us—some are even toxic. In his blog, "7 Smart Ways to Deal with Toxic People," Marc Chernoff (2013) describes "toxic bullies...that inflict enduring abuse and misery. If you observe these people closely, you will notice that their attitude is overly self-referential."

So, positive relationships are important, but they take skill and intentionality to identify and develop. As part of my self-care plan, I began increasing my awareness of the impact of relationships. At the end of this entry, I list selected resources that informed my thinking. As I developed managing relationships as a professional self-care skill, I have benefited by thinking of it as cultivating a self-care relationship garden. Please, allow me to share what I mean.

Weeds

Some people are good at producing a lot of negativity and little else. In the self-care garden, these people are like weeds that pull beneficial nutrients from the surrounding soil, making it almost impossible for anything of value to grow. You know the type. From the moment the staff meeting begins until it ends, weeds suck the creative energy from the room by only focusing on the negative; with any proposed program change, weeds only have unproductive complaints. When office gossip is circulating, weeds are the first to pull you aside to keep it going. Weeds create negative spaces, which are destructive to self-care.

I have discovered that I must limit my time with these folks—in both my professional and personal life. Part of my self-care plan is to set personal time limits for these individuals. If a weed-relationship asks to speak with me, I only give about five or ten minutes of my time. These hard boundaries are important not only to stop toxic people from spreading a culture of negativity, but also to maintain one's own positive outlook—essential for maintaining self-care.

Gnomes

Other relationships in the self-care garden are like gnomes. These are the people who offer a facade of support, but they do not really take the time to listen or provide any critical input that leads to growth. Gnome-relationships can take time to identify. I experienced a gnome-relationship in a practicum placement. A staff person in the agency expressed an interest in helping with a program with which I was working. During our third meeting together, I was met by the same seemingly eager person who expressed her willingness to help. Yet, she had not followed through with any mutually agreed upon goals.

Gnomes enhance the garden by making it whimsical, but their faces are fixed always in the same position. At the end of the day, they do not help to grow even one plant in your garden. Gnome-relationships always seem promising, but they leave you with nothing to show and can be deeply frustrating. Self-care is supported when we pay attention to people's actions *and* inactions. In other words, "Gnome" who they are! "Weed" them out! Don't set yourself up for frustration and disappointment by expecting them to be someone else or thinking you can change them.

Roses

Then there are roses—people who genuinely care, listen, and give the kind of feedback that is timely and beneficial. They want the best for you and take the time to show it, and the more time you spend with them, the more these relationships become reciprocal. These are the kind of relationships we need the most. At times, rose-relationships can be challenging, but in the most positive way. Care of an actual rose is not always easy; sometimes it even hurts. Roses can be thorny and need extra attention. But the time and energy is worth the effort, as they give back beautiful colors and fragrant smells. Rose-relationships give critical feedback that helps us grow. And, with growth, we are less susceptible to burnout, because we have cultivated the skills and wisdom to navigate more stressful days. We are rooted in healthy relationships.

During my first semester of graduate studies—amidst personal responsibilities, work, practicum, and homework—I neglected the time I needed to connect with my rose-relationships. My health and overall well-being showed this strain. So, I developed a self-care plan goal of scheduled times with friends, family, and colleagues who are my rose-relationships. The challenge came when I thought about spending time with my rose-relationships. My mind quickly brought up all the assignments and responsibilities I had limited time to accomplish. I discovered with practice, however, that when I spend adequate time with rose-relationships, I am actually more creative in my approach to my studies and work. In the end, I am more productive in my study time, and the quality of my work is even better. Win, Win—and roses, too!

In conclusion, all relationships take time and effort, but not all relationships are worth the same amount of time and effort. Developing strategies to cultivate relationships has helped me achieve better self-care. Evaluating my relationships through this self-care garden lens has helped me to identify weeds, gnomes, and roses in both my professional and personal life. Now, I set firm boundaries with certain people and have more time to be inspired by others. I hope that, as you consider your own relationships and self-care goals, you will take the time to "smell the roses" that appear on your garden path!

Reflection/Discussion

1. Think about the weeds and gnomes in your self-care garden. What are some practical self-care techniques you can use to limit the toxic effect of these relationships?
2. Rose-relationships need to be cultivated and nurtured to stay strong and life-giving. What specific steps can you take, in your own self-care plan, to cultivate and strengthen these relationships? (Example: I make it a practice to find small practical ways to show my gratitude. Part of my self-care plan is to send an email or card of thanks to a rose-relationship at least once a week.)

Selected Resources

Caprino, K. (2014, March 25). 3 signs someone is toxic (and 3 ways to keep them out of your life). Retrieved from *http://www.huffingtonpost.com/kathy-caprino/3-signs-someone-is-toxic-and-3-ways-to-keep-them-out-of-your-life_b_5024260.html*

Chernoff, M. (2013, Dec. 8). 7 smart ways to deal with toxic people. Retrieved from *http://www.marcandangel.com/2013/12/08/7-smart-ways-to-deal-with-toxic-people/*

Roffey, S. (Ed.). (2012). *Positive relationships: Evidence based practice across the world.* Dordrecht, Netherlands: Springer.

Supervision
Tiffany Dulamal

Treadmills, sleep, and dark leafy greens... self-care plans are often made of these. When we think about taking time for ourselves, our aspirations for exercise, rest, and diet often take place outside the work environment. However, self-care and office hours are not mutually exclusive. In addition to broader professional development (see *Professional Development* entry), supervision is an essential way to care for ourselves professionally. In a peer supervision spirit, I want to share with you what I have learned about this important element of self-care. Let's talk.

Benefits and Functions of Supervision

Cox and Steiner (2013) summarized the impact of supervision, citing studies that found a correlation between burnout and inadequate supervision. Likewise, adequate supervision is linked with several positive indicators, such as increased job satisfaction and reduced burnout. Also, they noted that quality supervision is related to positive client outcomes and satisfaction.

Maclean (2011) listed four functions of supervision: supportive, accountability, mediation, and developmental functions. A supervisor's *supportive* function includes providing professional support for supervisees. This function may include giving advice or training to increase supervisees' competency with the tasks required in their roles. The *accountability* function places supervisors in a managerial role, making sure that as a representative of the agency, supervisees are providing competent care to clients. The *mediation* function of the supervisor includes the task of helping individuals engage in the organization. This function may include teaching about how the agency is run and clarifying organizational requirements. Finally, in the *developmental* function, the supervisor should go beyond supporting the worker's role to support the worker's growth as a professional. Supervision is, therefore, a multi-faceted experience that nurtures the skills, self awareness, and even way of thinking for students and professionals.

Learning From Supervision

Sincero (2013) wrote, "If you're serious about changing your life, you'll find a way. If you're not, you'll find an excuse" (p. 151). This statement applies well to supervision. If our goal is truly to become better at our work, we must be dedicated enough to our self-improvement to find out what needs fine-tuning. As helping professionals, we use ourselves as tools in our work. Every now and then, we need to improve ourselves so we can do our best work and produce desirable outcomes.

However, hearing your supervisor tell you your shortcomings can be difficult. You may find yourself becoming defensive and feeling hurt by critical comments. I disclosed to my practicum supervisor my extreme discomfort with facilitating an addictions recovery group. I told him that I felt I was not providing adequate treatment because I did not feel knowledgeable enough.

He responded, "It sounds like you've gone all your life trying to be perfect, and you've done it by finding a 'formula' to get the right answer. It's worked for you in a lot of ways, probably with school and with research. Now that you're facilitating client groups, there is no formula, and that scares you. Working with our clients, there is no single formula, and you need to learn to be okay with that. You need to be okay with the fact that you are not perfect."

Wow! I had come to him for advice about how to lead a group, and suddenly he was in my head psychoanalyzing me! I was taken aback at first, but over time I saw how useful this insight was for me. I *did* have a drive to get absolutely everything right, and I had not thought about how this drive might negatively affect my work. We certainly do not expect our clients to be perfect. So, what business do we have expecting that of ourselves? Since then, I have been more conscious of when I am focusing more on perfection than being mentally present with my clients or other aspects of my work.

Mistakes have their consequences, but using supervision to learn from our mistakes empowers us to make better decisions in the future. As we learn from those mistakes and embrace those lessons, we begin to approach our work with confidence in our skills and humility in our areas of growth. Giving ourselves the opportunity to feel this way about ourselves is a part of self-care that is just as important as an exercise regimen or healthy diet.

Using Peer Supervision and Outside Mentorship

Regrettably, at times, those assigned to supervisory roles do not have the training or aptitude for the role. Sometimes, the supervisor's style may be a poor match for what you need. It's important for you to consider what you need from supervision.

Fortunately, direct supervisors are not the only sources of supervision that you can seek. Your peers in the workplace and trusted mentors inside or outside the workplace can often relate to what you are going through, allowing you a safe space to vent and address your stress. Sometimes their different perspectives can bring fresh insight. Other times, you feel safer talking to someone who does not hold authority over you. These peer or mentor connections can be just as important as the one you have with your supervisor.

Peers—whether other student interns or people who hold the same job description—encounter struggles similar to yours. They understand why the paperwork is so confusing or why that one client gets on your nerves. They may have learned how to deal with that frustrating computer problem. Collegial communication with your peers not only surrounds you with friendly contact, but gives you access to help and support when you need it. Group supervision or peer support groups can also be helpful, as they allow for mutual support and other advantages.

Mentors can help us set standards for ourselves, provide a listening ear, and give us hope and guidance. Personally, I enjoy having an outside mentor. Mine is a supervisor from a past internship in my hometown. After a particularly difficult and discouraging semester at my practicum placement, I confided in her my frustrations associated with working with "resistant" therapy clients. She listened patiently; when I finished, she laughed and validated those frustrations. She told me about her similar experiences and how she found the motivation to keep going. Hearing that my mentor (who is both a social worker and a nun) felt these negative feelings allowed me to step back and realize that, despite such frustrations, I can be a compassionate, effective social worker.

Let's not forget that supervisors need to be supported, as well. Cox and Steiner (2013) advised that supervisors address their stress through getting training on how to do supervision, learning conflict management skills, and maintaining professional boundaries. Also, they recommend peer support groups for supervisors and ongoing training. At every level, quality supervision is necessary to organizational wellness and practitioner self-care.

In conclusion, supervision is far more than a requirement for practicum or licensure or someone to do annual evaluations. Supervision provides an excellent, ongoing opportunity to receive the professional and emotional support that is essential in a profession particularly susceptible to burnout. It allows a safe space to explore areas of improvement and can renew our drive to help others. So, while planning a low-carb diet and finally scheduling that kickboxing class, make sure you get that hour of supervision, too. You deserve it!

Reflection/Discussion

1. What are your strengths and "areas of improvement"? How can a conversation with your supervisor help you draw on your strengths and increase your competency in growth areas?
2. What do you need in supervision? How might you go about getting that type of supervision?
3. Do you use peer consultation or mentorship? If so, how has it helped you in your practice? If not, how might you seek mentorship or peer consultation?

Selected Resources

Cox, K., & Steiner, S. (2013) *Self-care in social work: A guide for practitioners, supervisors, and administrators.* Washington, DC: NASW Press.

Maclean, S. (2013). *The social work pocket guide to stress and burnout.* Lichfield, Staffordshire, England: Kirwin Maclean and Associates, LTD.

Sincero, J. (2013). *You are a badass: How to stop doubting your greatness and start living an awesome life.* Philadelphia, PA: Running Press.

Time: More Than Just Managing
Tiffany Thompson

Time…I was feeling as if I had wasted too much time. I am not getting any younger. I am a wife and a mother of two teenagers. When I began the MSW program, I was completely unprepared for the level of intensity and time required to be successful. I was working full time, attending classes every other weekend, and completing practicum hours—all while trying to maintain a sense of balance and sanity. I was overworked, underpaid, sleep deprived, and getting older every second. I felt as if I never had "enough time." Unfortunately, I am not alone. Maclean (2011) notes that practitioners list the feeling of pressure related to time as a primary stressor.

After talking in some of my classes about self-care, I knew that I must make time–for me. I started looking for time management strategies. And I began to change the way I related to time.

Time Management 101

I came to realize that part of the curriculum had to be time management. Effective time management is essential to academic success and social work practice. Failure to utilize time management tools can result in missed deadlines, poor grades, stress, and compassion fatigue.

Similar to other new graduate students, I had a hard time meeting my academic, professional, and personal obligations. I would awaken after four to five hours of sleep, have some coffee, and begin the daily commute. I would drop the kids off at school, work my practicum hours, pick the kids up from school, prepare dinner, fit in family and schoolwork, and proceed to my job. After working a shift, I would drive home bleary-eyed, shower, crawl into bed, and hopefully live to do it again.

My time management skills needed some tweaking, to make sense of this immense burden I was carrying. I began by asking my cohort members what techniques they used to stay organized amid the multiple deadlines. As cohort members, we shared time management ideas via Facebook, email, text, or discussion board posts. By sharing our tips and tricks with each other, we fostered a sense of high support and accountability.

Some time management tips that we shared as a student cohort are:

- start a cohort Facebook group to share ideas, clarify questions, divide tasks, and give support;
- keep a binder with tabs for each subject;
- block out time for family and self-care;
- maintain schedules with room for flexibility;
- use digital alarms on phone or tablet;
- keep a daily planner book of assignments and meetings; and
- have a critical friend for accountability and moral support.

This resource sharing was invaluable. But I have learned that what works for others may not work for me. So, first, I had to get a good handle on my schedule and test out some strategies. After changing jobs three times during graduate school, I was able to get a job that allowed me to get more sleep. Instead of four to five choice hours, I gradually increased to six to eight hours of sleep.

Also, I started organizing my time and tasks. I kept a separate folder for each class. Whenever I had time to complete assignments during work or practicum, I seized the opportunity. By completing assignments ahead of time and throughout the day, I had less to do when I got home. I checked my email regularly and at a time when I could focus, in the morning. This strategy helped me stay abreast of assignments and course updates.

I made lists of tasks I needed to complete, checking them off as I completed them. I always try to keep appointment times, calling ahead if I need to reschedule. And I saved important dates for meetings and assignments on my digital calendar, which provided an audible reminder of what I needed to accomplish each day.

I also prioritized and blocked out time each day for family. I started being more mindful of including self-care in my daily routine. I started exercising at least three times per week for 50 minutes per session. I began drinking protein smoothies (12 oz.) for breakfast, five days a week, in the morning instead of grabbing something on the go. I enjoy a manicure and/or pedicure every two weeks, which takes about 30 minutes per visit. Anticipating self-care each week improves my self-esteem and my outlook on life.

Finally, I learned the importance of "making time" for support. As MSW students, we all recognized that we needed each other to successfully complete this program. The cohort members that I grew close to helped me stay focused, organized, and encouraged. I contact friends on a weekly basis via text, email, and phone. I am careful to process my problems and critically think about solutions throughout the day. I try to have healthy conversations daily. I have a couple of critical friends who provide moral support when I am feeling overwhelmed by all of my responsibilities.

Time management created a feasible work schedule, allowing space for assignments, online time, practicum hours, family/friends, and self-care. Using time management tools, I began to feel more organized, less frustrated, and more at peace with my busy lifestyle and the people I encounter. Using these time management tips gave me a sense of relief as I continued along my academic journey and began my professional path.

Time-Shifting and Understanding Time in a Cultural Context

As I worked on time management, I also began learning about the importance of my perception of time. In our culture, we sometimes view time as an enemy; time is viewed as something out of our control. When we think about all of the responsibilities we have and the places we have to go, it is easy to feel burdened. However, I began to realize the importance of reframing time as a gift to be savored, rather than a commodity to be managed or saved (Grise-Owens, 1998). We need to learn to embrace each day and enjoy each moment. (See *Mindfulness* entry.) Bass (2000) is a helpful resource for spiritual practices for learning about the gift of time. Also, Rechtschaffen (1996) provides six categories for "time-shifting." These include:

- being in the moment;
- creating time boundaries;
- honoring the mundane;
- creating spontaneous time;
- doing what we like to do; and
- creating time retreats.

As social workers, we recognize the relationship between personal concerns and broader systemic issues. In my MSW program, I learned about how *time* is a social concern; that is, time affects much of our social and cultural structures (Grise-Owens, Miller, & Owens, 2014). For example, the U.S. ranks low in comparison to other comparable countries in areas such as vacation time, living wage, and family leave. The Take Back Your Time (TBYT) movement addresses these concerns. Check out the website (TBYT, n.d.) for information and resources, such as publications (e.g., deGraaf, 2003) and other media, such as documentaries.

As part of a self-care plan, I have developed better time management skills. Beyond managing, I have recognized the need to relate to time in a healthier way—including an awareness of time in the cultural context. These changes help me be more at peace with what I have accomplished at the end of the day. This approach keeps me from becoming overwhelmed and reminds me that life is precious and must be savored.

Reflection/Discussion

1. What is your relationship with time? Do you see time as a blessing or a burden? How might changing your relationship with/perception of time improve your self-care and wellness?

2. How are your own time management techniques beneficial? What areas need improvement?
3. What tips and techniques have you learned that help?
4. How can time management and time savoring be coupled with other self-care strategies to improve overall wellness?

Selected Resources

Bass, D. (2000). *Receiving the day.* San Francisco, CA: Jossey-Bass.

deGraaf, J. (2003). *Take back your time: Fighting overwork and time poverty.* San Francisco, CA: Berrett-Koehler.

Grise-Owens, E., Miller, J., & Owens, L. W. (2014). Responding to global shifts: "Meta"-practice as a relevant social work practice paradigm. *Journal of Teaching in Social Work, 34*(1), 46-59.

Grise-Owens, E. (1998). Time savoring: A timely topic for family ministry. *Family Ministry, 12*(3), 46-56.

Maclean, S. (2011). *The social work pocket guide to...stress and burnout.* Lichfield, Staffordshire, England: Kirwin Maclean Associates LTD.

Rechtschaffen, S. (1996). *Timeshifting: Creating more time to enjoy your life.* New York, NY: Doubleday.

Take Back Your Time. (n.d.). Retrieved from *https://www.takebackyourtime.org/*

U R Worth It
Donia Addison

Learning that I am worth engaging in self-care wasn't easy. In a society where employers are not required to provide paid vacations for employees, self-care is not a high priority in the United States (Mohn, 2013). Paid time off is not valued and, therefore, is not required. The modern norm is to go, go, go until you crash, crash, crash.

And crash is exactly what I did three years ago. While working a high stress, high demand job in social services, I nearly lost everything that was important to me. I hope that by sharing my discovery of the critical need for self-care, you will also recognize a need in your own life. With a sense of worthiness for self-care and priority setting, we can all lead less stressed and more productive lives.

Discovering My Worth

My grandmother always said, "Sweet Cake, stress will kill you." She was almost right. I worked so much that I did not take time for my family or myself. My health began to deteriorate. For most of my adult life, I had lived with migraines. But, increasingly, they came more often and the intensity was worse each time. As a result, I began to evaluate the role my job was playing in the condition of my health and neglect for self-care.

I began to ponder what brought me to this point. Why had I neglected my family and my health? At the time, self-care was not on my radar. My day was filled with a stressful and never-ending job that often took over my nights and weekends. I did not feel I was worth engaging in "me time." I had a small child, worked, and had a husband. Being in a helping profession, such as social work, I suspect I was not alone in putting self-care on the back burner.

Shaw (2013) discussed mothers being first responders and needing to engage in self-care/me time in order to respond well. Further, Shaw said we are more responsive and enjoyable to be around when we take time for ourselves. This information is also true for social workers. Often, social workers are the first responders to very complex issues and, therefore, should strive to maintain a level of balance to best serve clients in their time of greatest need. In her blog, Goldman (2013) wrote, "If everyone else around you is worthy of care and attention, then, so are you." (See *Awareness* entry regarding self-compassion.)

After realizing my health and closest relationships were in shambles, I began a journey of restoration. I vowed that I would never take my family or my life for granted again. Although the start of my journey began with the evaluation of my health and stressful job, self-care came to fruition in my first year as a social work graduate student. In the MSW program, I began to develop the skills needed in self-care and cultivating a self-care plan that was SMART (specific, measurable, achievable, realistic, and time limited). (See *Appendix A—Self-Care Planning Form.*) Implementing a plan, I soon learned the importance of prioritizing self-care.

Learning to POP:
Prioritize, Organize, and Partialize

Learning to prioritize isn't an easy task, either. Priority setting is not just about how and when to complete tasks. Priority setting is also about making *myself* a priority and not feeling guilty about it. Goldman (2013) suggests setting aside 15-30 minutes daily to make "you" a priority. This prioritizing can be reading a book, taking a walk, or watching your favorite television show. When I take time for myself, I am present in mind, body, and spirit—not just physically. I am able to truly enjoy my family, and they enjoy me.

Prioritizing is also about the inevitable array of tasks we must complete. From going to the grocery store to completing labor-intensive assignments for graduate school, I prioritize my commitments and activities. Grise-Owens (2008) provides helpful advice for graduate students seeking a degree in social work; she uses the acronym "POP" (prioritize, organize, and partialize). This advice is applicable to everyone, not just students seeking a degree in social work.

I organize! I put activities on my planner. I make lists for meetings, assignments, deadlines, and even my daughter's activities. I partialize! I break assignments, work projects, and home projects into increments so they are not as over-whelming. I prioritize! This prioritizing includes *scheduling self-care,* including time for myself to catch up with friends and family. It is part of my self-care plan. (See *Yes List* entry for more discussion on this idea.)

My experience in being a mom, wife, employee, and student may differ somewhat from others' experiences. Leading a stressful life is not restricted to married individuals with children; everyone leads busy, stressful lives. To some degree, it is the nature of the society in which we live. Social workers need to recognize the necessity of taking care of ourselves to better take care of those we serve.

Each of us is on a journey to discover one's self-worth in self-care. My journey took some twists and turns. But, in the end, I realized that self-care allows me to be a better mother, wife, social worker, citizen, friend, daughter, and sister. When I take time for myself, I am refreshed, focused, and present.

I learned that setting priorities begins with making myself a priority. Not taking time for ourselves causes us to be out of balance and lose sight of what is really important in life (Goldman, 2013). Cooper (2015) emphasizes the importance of discipline and prioritization in dealing with the "busyness" of our lives. For me, an excellent week in self-care is being prepared, organized, and tackling projects incrementally. Self-care is what each of us makes of it. I hope sharing my experience can encourage you to realize UR worth it!

Reflection/Discussion

1. What will it take for you to realize UR worthy of self-care?
2. Are your priorities aligned the way you would like? Have you made yourself a priority? Are you ready to make self-care a priority?
3. How can you prioritize, organize, and partialize?

Selected Resources

Cooper, A. (2015). Why I'm so busy. Retrieved from *http:// www.socialworker.com/extras/social-work-month-2015/why- so-busy/*

Goldman, E. (2013, October 25). 8 ways to put yourself on your priority list: Finding time for "me" time. SparkPeople. com. Retrieved from *http://www.sparkpeople.com/resource/ wellness_articles.asp?id=1657*

Grise-Owens, E. (2008). Traveling toward a social work degree: 10 road-tested trip-tips. *The New Social Worker Magazine.* Retrieved from *http://www.socialworker.com/ feature-articles/education–credentials/Traveling_Toward_a_ Social_Work_Degree%3A_10_Road-Tested_Trip-Tips/*

Mohn, T. (2013, August 13). U.S. the only advanced economy that does not require employers to provide paid vacation time, report says. *Forbes.* Retrieved from *http://www. forbes.com/sites/tanyamohn/2013/08/13/paid-time-off- forget-about-it-a-report-looks-at-how-the-u-s-compares-to-other- countries/#7165c2d2bd8a*

Shaw, G. (2013, September 24). A woman's guide to 'me' time: How to find the time for yourself and why it matters. WebMD. Retrieved from *http://www.webmd.com/women/ guide/womans-guide-to-me-time*

Values—Reflections on Who I Am and Why I'm a Social Worker
Vickie L. Thompson

We do not learn core values from books; our parents, families, and community teach us. As we develop, so do our values. Social workers' values are intertwined in our daily practice.

Mirror, Mirror: Reflections on Losing Myself

I became a social worker to advocate for social justice and, like most other social workers, to "save the world." Quickly, I realized the importance of self-awareness and reflection on my own values when working with clients. Always respecting clients and their values is a core social work principle.

I want to look in the mirror and know the person looking back at me is implementing the values of social work. My personal and professional values are challenged daily, in an atmosphere of rampant negativity, complacency, and pessimism within my public child welfare agency. The demands of bureaucratic agency policies, lack of supervisory support, and minimal resources for the clients we serve creates a climate of anxiety and stress. This climate began to affect every aspect of my life, including my attitude with clients, my family, and friends.

I lost "myself" at some point. I let the environment of the agency change who I was and influence my values and beliefs. I allowed "garbage" to affect my thinking and interfere with my ability to help my clients. I became discouraged and disconnected from my original zeal.

The person staring back at me in the mirror scared me, because she was not me. She had forgotten how values play such an important part in practice. She did not know how to balance professional and personal life.

Mirror, Mirror: Reflections on Self-Care and Ethical Practice

I had no idea what a self-care plan was or how to implement one in my daily life. I just knew my values were deteriorating quickly. I was not sure who I was any more. I heard team members talk about self-care, but it was not something I understood how to do until I began the MSW program. After learning about self-care and reflecting on the initial stress I felt when I began working for my agency, I am not sure how I made it.

I realized early in the MSW program the importance of a SMART self-care plan. In developing my self-care plan, I became more focused on my values. In turn, I realized how important it was to understand the impact my values had on every aspect of my life. When I reflect on my personal values and those we aspire to as social workers, although I might state them differently, they are very similar in content. I believe in social justice and equality for all. I believe in respecting the inherent dignity and worth of all people and embracing diversity. I live by authenticity in every aspect of my life, because it builds trust. With trust, strong relationships grow. I live to serve others and advocate for those who are in need. I value life, liberty, and justice for all and value having the ability to practice social work in a competent manner. Values are important to our personal lives. Holding onto our values is equally important in our professional lives. I am fortunate to be able to express my values in practice without limiting who I am as a person.

Upholding our values and advocating for the oppressed and most vulnerable in our society can affect us, emotionally, and in every aspect of life. As our values are tested and tried, we are stretched to our limits sometimes. I understand why NASW (2008) implores social workers to practice self-care, as an ethical obligation. Taking care of ourselves is a way of taking care of our clients. When we feel the stress of burnout or secondary traumatic stress, we will not work competently or effectively with our clients. Dolan (2015) emphasizes the importance of reconnecting to what compelled us to the join the profession and using this connection to sustain us in the profession. I have found that a SMART self-care plan helps with keeping me on track.

Reflections: Mirror, Mirror, What Might Be?

I have learned that reflection is an important part of self-care. Reflection helps me be more aware of the value conflicts, as well as the congruency with my values, in my job. Biggs (as cited in Maclean, 2010) said, "A reflection in a mirror is an exact replica of what is in front of it. Reflection in professional practice, however, gives back not what it is, but what it *might be,* an improvement of the original" (p. 9). Maclean recommends several strategies and processes for reflection as integral to professional practice, including keeping a professional reflection journal.

I have found this practice of journaling very helpful. I write out the negative and positive aspects of my days. I write about the negatives to release them and start over. I write about the positives to reinforce my mission and purpose. In self-care, no single day will ruin the whole plan. If you value your plan and you make a mistake, then write away the mistake through reflecting. Then, jump back in and start over with new motivation.

Another way I reflect is through taking a timeout. I take a few minutes to regroup when things get tough. I sit at my desk or in my car. I close my eyes and let my mind drift off for a few minutes to a place where there is no clutter. And I breathe. Once I feel calmer, usually about five minutes later, I go back to whatever I need to do. I have found I am more productive and much more focused.

Practicing self-care through reflection and remembering who I am and what I stand for makes me stronger as a social worker. I am more focused for my clients, my own family, and myself. I have learned self-care will only make me a better person all around. It helps me maintain my values, grow as a social worker, and sustain the authentic person I have always been. Values make us who we are as social workers—and as human beings. Valuing and implementing self-care makes us more ethical practitioners who are able to advocate for ourselves, our families, our clients, our causes, and the community as a whole. By valuing self-care, we can mirror the wellness we wish to create in the world. Indeed, through reflective self-care, we can give back what *might be.*

Reflection/Discussion

1. What are some of your core values, and how do they relate to the profession's values? Have you experienced times of "losing yourself" and your core values? How do your values relate to self-care?
2. What strategies and processes do you already use or might you incorporate for reflection? What *might be* the outcomes of this reflection?
3. Consider how self-care is an ethical obligation. What does this consideration mean for your practice?

Selected Resources

Dolan, A. (2015). Supporting social workers in our life-changing work. Retrieved from *http://www.socialworker. com/extras/social-work-month-2015/supporting-social-workers-in-our-life-changing-work/*

National Association of Social Workers. (2008). Professional self-care and social work. In NASW, *Social work speaks: NASW policy statement 2009-2012* (pp. 268-272). Washington, DC: Author.

Maclean, S. (2010). *The social work pocket guide to...reflective practice.* Lichfield, Staffordshire, England: Kirwin Maclean Associates.

Workspace
Jillian Harlamert & Geneva White

In our field, work environments can be very stressful. The high stress is due to many factors, such as trauma we witness and hear about, high volume of caseloads, and disrespect from clients and the community. Unfortunately, our own workspace can be an additional stress.

Working with people who have different work styles and personalities can be challenging. Some people like to be very social at work and talk throughout the day; others isolate from the group. Being a social butterfly can cause you to get behind in your work, distract others, and display unprofessional boundaries. On the other hand, being a lonely recluse can create a negative perception, cause tension between you and your co-workers, and isolate you from critical friends and much needed support. In addition to these social factors, physical factors affect the quality of the workspace.

We (Geneva and Jillian) have worked together for the past three years for the Cabinet for Health and Family Services on the same Child Protective Service Team in Louisville, KY. We also attended the same MSW program at Spalding University. We have developed a strong professional friendship. In this entry, we will share six self-care tips that we have incorporated to create a positive, fun, and professional workspace!

Tip #1: Do an Environmental Scan

As social workers, we know the client's environment matters. However, too often, we become so accustomed to *our* environment that we do not even think of the stress it may contribute. So, do an environmental scan of your workspace and workflow this week. Notice when you are frustrated, distracted, or uncomfortable. Similarly, notice what helps you feel comfortable, focused, and positive.

What factors—even small, seemingly insignificant ones—influence your work environment? Think of how you can accentuate the positives and minimize the negatives. Each person's list may differ, but the key is to raise your awareness and take proactive steps to make changes.

Tip #2: Change Your Workspace

Norcross (2000) recommends self-renewal as a strategy for self-care (p. 4). He suggests diversifying your work environment by changing positions, alternating the type of work you do, or varying the population with whom you work. For example, both of us have used this technique to avoid burnout. I (Geneva) worked at a hospital for 10 years; changing positions within the hospital every two to three years helped me prevent burnout. This movement kept me engaged, motivated, and excited for a new challenge. However, if you are averse to that much change, simply moving from one office to an open office space down the hall or switching with a co-worker can provide a fresh perspective.

I (Jillian) diversified my workspace by moving from one county within my agency to another county. I worked in the first county for two years and after a while was feeling a strong sense of burnout. Before I decided to quit my job completely, I wanted to change up my workspace by transferring to another county. After the move, I felt rejuvenated and have stayed for another three years—free from burnout!

Similarly, at Geneva's current position with Child Protective Services (CPS), my original office was at the end of the hallway in a closed off cubicle. As an extrovert, I felt as if I was missing out and felt isolated from my teammates. I took charge of my workspace; I requested a move to the open desk inside the pod area where two of my co-workers, including Jillian, had desks. This simple move made a huge difference for me. I felt as if I had more support from my teammates; I was actually able to concentrate better in an open area. It was also easier for me to reach out for help in the pod than when I was secluded in the other office.

On the other hand, introverts may have a different need. You may feel distracted by a busy, open workspace.

You may want to have more boundaries in your workspace, while balancing connections. Part of your self-care plan is knowing yourself and what type of workspace best fits your personality.

Tip #3: Make It YOUR Space

Not every workplace is going to be conducive to a positive atmosphere. Sometimes, you just have to make your workspace work for you. We find it helpful to personalize our workspace by decorating it with pictures of friends, family, children, and people who have had an impact on us throughout our careers. When we are having a rough day, looking at these pictures reminds us why we continue to do this hard job day in and day out. We make our workspace comfortable by decorating it as we do our own homes. Our building management prohibits open flames, but we use candle warmers to fill our space with fresh aromas. These touches bring a little bit of home to the office and make coming to work more enjoyable.

You may not be comfortable with this level of personal exposure in your workspace, but think through what will make your workspace YOURS. You may want to have some photos from places you have travelled, nature scenes, inspiring quotes, or live plants. Think of all your senses; sight, smell, hearing, taste, and touch. Consider having elements in your workspace that consider all the senses. No matter how large or limited your workspace, put your personal stamp there. Make it a pleasant and peaceful place to be… for YOU, as well as others.

Tip #4: Get Organized

Typically, resources on creating a positive, productive, and peaceful workspace recommend organizing strategies. For example, Garrett (n.d.) makes suggestions such as, "Wipe the slate clean to get serene," and "Clear the clutter." I (Jillian) find it especially helpful to have an organized workspace. Being organized helps clear my mind and keeps me focused on the next task. Being organized helps me keep up with deadlines and improves time management and work performance. When I moved to the pod, I de-cluttered the workspace by purging old files and outdated materials. You can turn on music and make this organizing a fun team effort.

Again, personal style has an impact on one's attention to and even definition of organization. Consider the flow of your workday. What changes might help you organize so that your flow goes more smoothly for you?

Tip #5: Have an In-Office Day

Social work and related jobs can be very chaotic. Seemingly, we are always on the go. Therefore, setting aside one day out of the week to stay in the office to do paperwork has been very beneficial for us. On this day, we turn off our phones, put our "away" message on our emails, and put on headphones to avoid any distraction. I (Jillian) listen to calm relaxing music. I have found the "Calm Meditation Radio" channel on Pandora or anything instrumental to be most helpful.

Organizing a team office day can make this day fun! The team can make it festive by having a potluck with everyone bringing in a favorite dish to share or by ordering pizza. With everyone's hectic schedules, it can sometimes be hard to eat lunch together as a team. But this day allows time for everyone to be available and spend time together. Taking these breaks and decompressing with teammates is imperative for good self-care.

Tip #6: Create a Supportive Environment

Sometimes in our work, we need to laugh to keep from crying. We hear and see things on a daily basis that other people cannot even imagine. Finding laughter and humor in the workplace can be a major stress reliever, especially on those days when the work is unbearable. We recall one day when the team was working a half day. After a stressful and long week, we happily anticipated a free Friday afternoon.

Right before leaving, I (Geneva) called a client to schedule a home visit for the following week. When I dialed the client's number, her ring back tone's music prompted my supervisor and me to start a dance party. Distracted with dancing, we did not realize when the music stopped, and the client answered the phone. She said "hello" several times before we left our dance party and came back to reality. Regaining composure, I scheduled the home visit. Embarrassed in the moment, we still laugh about it today.

In this field, we can encounter so much negative energy from our clients and the community, we must support each other in our workplace. Offering a listening ear when a co-worker needs to vent, debriefing after stressful days at court, helping cover visits and appointments for each other, and even having an impromptu dance party will create a supportive climate. This climate reduces the stress in this job. Someone is always there in a time of need.

These six simple self-care tips will improve the quality of your practice and reduce stress in your workspace. Whether you are new in the field or an experienced veteran, self-care is essential to maintain your well-being. Your workspace makes a significant difference in your morale. Use these tips to create a positive, fun, and professional environment. Use your own environmental scan and your imagination to determine what is most beneficial for your workspace!

Reflection/Discussion

1. Think about your own workspace. Do you prefer to be the recluse or the butterfly? Are you more an introvert or extrovert? How does this affect your relationships in the workplace?
2. How do you relieve stress in your workplace? How can you incorporate stress reduction into an ongoing self-care plan?
3. Think of ways that you can engage your co-workers in your self-care plan (e.g., cleaning out old files, motivational music, and creating a team in-office day).

Selected Resources

Garrett, L. (n.d.). 6 ways to create a more peaceful work-space. *Gaiam Life.* Retrieved from *http://life.gaiam.com/article/6-ways-create-more-peaceful-workspace*

Norcross, J. C. (2000). Psychotherapist self-care: Practitioner-tested, research-informed strategies. *Professional Psychology: Research and Practice, 31*(6), 710-713.

eXpressive Arts
Kimberly Crum

In her frequently anthologized essay, *In Search of Our Mother's Gardens,* novelist Alice Walker mourns and celebrates the creativity of poor Black women from slavery to the Reconstruction, and beyond. She describes how these women who were "the mules of the world" were compelled to write poetry, sing the blues, tell stories, sew quilts, and plant gardens (as cited in Mitchell, 1994, p. 401). Walker writes about the slave girl, Phyllis Wheatley, abducted as a child from her native Africa, whose poetry is now revered. She describes the Gee's Bend, Alabama, quilts, sewn from work clothes and scraps, vivid in color and design—simple utilitarian bed-coverings until they were designated as "art" in the 1990s.

While many of these endeavors were required work tasks, the women created enjoyment. The process of creation satisfied their souls. They did not expect recognition or reward.

Creativity in Ordinary Days

Self-care is sometimes portrayed as a form of recreation—what you will finally *do for yourself* when the clients, the family, and home cease their various demands. But the creative endeavors Walker describes were both practical and life giving—folded into ordinary days. For today's hard working professionals, creative processes might begin during lunch, at a gas station, in the line at the grocery store, between client visits, in an office, with small children, or in the early hours of the day. Here are a few questions you might be asking:

- How do I recognize "soul work" that energizes?
- Must I be artistic or talented?
- What "scraps" of my life can I quilt into words, image, or song?

Psychologist Rollo May (as cited in Paintner, 2007) described creativity as "the process of bringing something new into being" (p. 2). One needs an imagination, not necessarily artistic talent, to create something new: an idea, a thank-you note, doodles on a clipboard, a poetic Tweet, or a journal entry. An important aspect of creativity is the emphasis on process over product. "When you create, surrendering to the process, you become fully present," according to Paintner (2007, p. 5). This concept is familiar to the social worker who, day after day, tries to be fully present for clients. The social worker (or other professional)—fatigued by continuous compassion—might crave to be "fully absent."

Writing as Self-Care

For this retired social worker, writing has always been part of my work and play—a meditative activity. In my current role, as a memoir teacher, I see these same effects with my students. I note that students devalue their writing skills and creativity at the start of a workshop, although each has a specific story to tell—often related to a traumatic life event. My first advice is to start writing about something that seems insignificant. Creative power is found in the smallest details of life. "When you can't make sense of the world in any other way, merely to describe what you see before you leads to understanding," according to Peacock (1999, p. 166). In the process of describing the "insignificant" details, many memoir writers see their stories in new ways. Putting story into writing, even trauma, provides a safe psychic distance from the event. In fact, our ethic in memoir group is to consider how the story is told, rather than to focus on the event itself. Memoir students revisit and revise their true stories.

In her blog essay, *Writing Your Way to Happiness,* journalist Parker-Pope (2015) discusses research that shows expressive writing has positive benefits among people with mood disorders and cancer (para. 1). A psychology professor at the University of Texas, Pennebaker, showed positive effects of expressive writing on perceived health among college students.

One poet describes the benefit of her writing habit: "The unexpected result of training your eye on detail is that the world becomes more beautiful simply because it is noticed" (Peacock, 1999, p. 167). As William Faulkner said, "A writer needs three things: experience, observation and imagination, any two of which...can supply the lack of the others" (Stein, 1956).

Using the Ordinary for New Connections and Creations

Writing is only one of the expressive arts. Music, visual arts, gardening, cooking, quilting, and all manner of crafts offer opportunities to use ordinary materials to create something new. As Walker observed, our ordinary activities can be opportunities for expressive creativity. Citing William Plomer, Brené Brown (2010) defined creativity as "the power to connect the seemingly unconnected" (p. 96). Brown observed how social work is about making connections; so, part of her "transformation was owning and celebrating my existing creativity" (p. 96).

Brown (2010) emphasized the importance of letting go of comparison, competition, and conformity, in order to engage in creativity. These habits squelch the freedom and flexibility necessary for open expression. Don't compare your expressive endeavors with others. Don't compete for attention or attribution, and don't conform to external expectations. Claim and celebrate your creativity!

To benefit from the expressive arts and engage creativity, no extra inspiration is necessary. Study your world. Ask a question. Describe a detail. Express yourself in the medium of your choice. Then, see what happens.

Reflection/Discussion

1. How might you integrate expressive creation into your "ordinary" days? What expressive arts appeal to you?
2. Try this 30-minute writing exercise as one way for self-expression:

a.   Designate a notebook that you will use for your writing. No lovely journals, please! Beautiful journals require beautiful writing. Your notebook should be ordinary enough for spontaneous thoughts and sentence fragments.

b.   Before each writing session, choose a focal point: an object, a quote, an image, a song lyric. Then set a timer for 30 minutes, and write continuously. When the alarm sounds, you may quit and close your notebook.

c.   Writing for less than 30 minutes is fine. Know that in the first 10 minutes of writing, you are merely warming up! But it's better to establish a habit for less than 30 minutes than to forgo the experience.

d.   Think of your notebook as a quilt and your entries as "scraps." One day, you might choose to review the scraps and assemble these scraps in a new way. Or not.

e.   Consider some additional writing prompts:
   • If my life were a song, it would be...
   • What I can't forget/What I'd like to remember
   • My first... (you fill in the blank!)
   • If my life were a quilt, it would be...
   • If my life flashed before my eyes, I would see...
   • A memory of a story told and embellished many times
   • A monologue in the voice of a friend, family member, or acquaintance.

Selected Resources

Brown, B. (2010). *The gifts of imperfection: Let go of who you think you're supposed to be and embrace who you are.* Center City, MN: Hazelden.

Paintner, C. V. (2007, January). The relationship between spirituality and artistic expression. *Spirituality in Higher Education Newsletter. 3*(2), 1-6. Retrieved from *http://spirituality.ucla.edu/docs/newsletters/3/Paintner_Jan07.pdf*

Parker-Pope, T. (2015, January 19). Writing your way to happiness. *The New York Times.* Retrieved from *http://well.blogs.nytimes.com/2015/01/19/writing-your-way-to-happiness/?_r=0*

Peacock, M. (1999). *How to read a poem...and start a poetry circle.* New York, NY: Riverhead Books.

Stein, J. (1956, Spring). William Faulkner: The art of fiction no. 12. *The Paris Review, 12.* Retrieved from *http://www.theparisreview.org/interviews/4954/the-art-of-fiction-no-12-william-faulkner*

Walker, A. (1994). In search of our mother's gardens. In A. Mitchell (Ed.). *Within the circle: An Anthology of African-American literary criticism from the Harlem Renaissance to the present,* pp. 401-409. Durham, NC, & London, England: Duke University Press. Retrieved from *https://www.uwosh.edu/african_am/aas-100-canon-materials/walker_in_search.pdf*

Yes (and No) Lists: Life-Long Learning
Kristin L. Johnson

When I first started my journey in becoming a social worker, I was terrified that I might have made the wrong choice. As I continued, I discovered very quickly it was the perfect choice. I love being an ally, empowering others, and pursuing social justice. The profession is amazing, and one of my favorite aspects is the opportunity to be a life-long learner. I love to learn and have a desire to take in as much as I can. However, with an eagerness to take in everything, I developed a habit of saying "Yes!" to everything and overloading my schedule.

Lesson Learned: Say "No" to say "YES!"

In my MSW program, I was learning that self-care is an important part of being a professional social worker. To help others, we must take care of ourselves first. With an overloaded schedule because of school, work, and family responsibilities, I started to wonder how I could continue to manage it all and find time for self-care. Honestly, I was barely managing my schedule and responsibilities. My self-care plan consisted of making sure I had at least five hours of sleep each night.

An overloaded schedule was not helping my clients, my family, or me. I decided to look more closely at this concern. Being an organized person, I wrote everything down in my planner. I left nothing out, writing down meetings, classes, coursework due dates, appointments, bill payments, family functions, and special days. Each day had at least one entry; some days had more. Seeing this depiction of my overcommitted life, I decided it was too much. I needed to reduce the number of entries and activities.

Being a visual person, I decided organizing my schedule by color would work best. I sat down with colored pens and used different colors to signify different activities. I used orange for work; green for practicum; brown for appointments; a different color for each course I was taking; and black for family, friends, and miscellaneous. I eliminated bill payments and put those in my phone as reoccurring reminders. This system made a difference in decluttering my schedule.

My next step was to question whether a scheduled activity was a priority or an option. I often feel compelled to attend meetings or other events because this participation is a privilege. However, maintaining this privilege is contingent on good self-care and being healthy enough to participate.

With a color-coded schedule, I felt organized and ready to say "No" so I could say "Yes." I had to figure out my starting point for my yes/no list. I looked to see which color had the most events. I had many things scheduled for work. Out of 20 working days in February, 14 of the days had a meeting or event scheduled. This schedule needed to change.

I have a caseload of 75 high school students who are at risk of dropping out of school. I focus on attendance, grades, classroom behavior, college and career readiness, and life skills. My caseload of students varies in age and grade. A big part of my job is attending various committee meetings within my school and the school district. Being in meetings pulls me away from managing my caseload. So, this prioritization was an important starting point. Some of the meetings were held weekly. I spoke with other team members, and we changed one meeting to bi-weekly, because we were already communicating nearly every day. With another weekly meeting, I decided I would only attend if the agenda related to concerns regarding my students.

Making small adjustments like these allowed three to four extra hours each week to manage my caseload. By saying "No" to meetings that were only sometimes beneficial in helping my students, I was able to spend more time focusing on student case plans and maintaining paperwork. After prioritizing work responsibilities and learning not to feel obligated, I felt some relief. I also began putting self-care activities (such as my mindfulness practice) on my schedule.

Morgenstern (2013) gives some helpful suggestions in creating a "saner to-do list." She asserts that a good to-do list *always* includes self-care strategies, such as connecting with friends or family, doing something for yourself (like working out), and anticipating mini-crises through leaving time cushions in your schedule. Likewise, she suggests breaking a large-scale project into smaller, less intimidating tasks; then, put one task at a time on your weekly to-do list. Furthermore, she advises winnowing out unrealistic or unhealthy expectations. For instance, she suggests figuring out which "To Do" items should just be deleted, such as calling for that coffee date with that person who really just saps your energy.

Similarly, Richardson (2009) advises creating an "absolute no list." Items might include "Not answering the phone during dinner" or "Not rushing." In that vein, a colleague told me that she and her sister have a "Stupid S*** I Don't Do Anymore (SSIDDA)" list. First on their SSIDDA list is "Not taking responsibility that belongs to someone else." They remind one another by using the code word: "SSIDDA!" I have learned that a "YES" life requires a "No" list!

Lesson Learned: I Can't Make Everyone Happy

At this point, you may be skeptically thinking, "Yeah, right! It is not that easy to say 'no' to say 'yes.'" So true! In balancing other obligations with school, practicum, and family, saying "No" was more complicated. I had to prioritize, plan, and be flexible when unforeseen activities arose. I learned this valuable lesson: I cannot make everyone happy. Sometimes people are going to be upset, disappointed, and even angry when told "No"—even when expressed in the most respectful and considerate way. I have learned the benefit of surrounding myself with compassionate and understanding individuals. These people will be more likely to accept that I am committed to fully saying "Yes"—which means I have to say "No" at times.

I am honest with family, friends, co-workers, and—yes—even my supervisors. I realize my limitations and time constraints. I try to be a person of my word and hold myself accountable. By saying "No" to some things, I am able to say "Yes" with commitment and confidence.

The hardest place to say "No" was at my practicum. I wanted to learn and experience it all. In planning my practicum schedule, I had to be mindful of staying within the frame of 12-15 hours a week. One month, I somehow put in 80 hours when the maximum I needed was 60. Many opportunities came to me, and I did not want to say "No."

Lesson Learned: Doing Nothing Is Necessary Sometimes

My biggest lesson came when not saying "No" resulted in my having to take an entire day to rest. Saying "Yes!" got me to a point where I was drained. Like many others, I was going nonstop! I got up at 5:00 a.m. to start my day and got home around 9:30 p.m. most days. I was skipping meals, not working out, and not getting adequate sleep.

But one day, I made a choice to do NOTHING—which turned out to be something important! I slept, I slept, and I slept some more—14 hours off and on, to be exact. And I needed it. The previous two weeks, I had struggled to stay awake and to remember simple things, like PIN numbers and pass-codes I used daily. This day, I decided everything could wait! Like a child who needs redirection and focus, I needed a TIMEOUT! I slept on and off all day, watched some TV, and then, finally, at 7 p.m., I reached a point at which I could do a little something. I cleaned my living room, kitchen, and bathroom, and that was it. I went to bed at 10 p.m. The next day, I felt much better. Sometimes we need reminding that whatever we have to do CAN AND WILL WAIT!

Yes, I had papers to write; yes, I needed to read; yes, I had chores to do. But I had to say "No" to help myself. I reached a point where I had nothing left, and that is not a good place to be as a social worker, family member, or friend. I reached a point of not caring and wanted to throw in the towel on graduate school. However, taking a timeout from responsibilities, getting some sleep, taking time to relax, and letting go of the never-ending "to-do" list rejuvenated me and lifted my mood. I have learned that "nothing" time is crucial.

Lesson Learned: Whole-Hearted Living Is Good Self-Care

We all have many reasons we hesitate to say "No." I have been making it part of my regular vocabulary. Reading *The Gift of Imperfection* by Brené Brown (2010), I discovered that I am a casualty to society's expectation of productivity. We live in a society that bases self-worth on how busy, successful, and productive you are. In reality, we are just validating our ability to overwork and carry stress. It is okay to say "No" and take time out to redirect and focus. Everything can wait! Fink-Samnick (2007) lists being conscious of our need for time out, being okay with pampering ourselves, and refusing to feel guilty about having fun as essential steps in fostering professional resilience. In articulating wholehearted living, Brown emphasizes that living and loving our whole self involves valuing our need for restoration. Play and sleep are important ways to rejuvenate. When I take time for play and sleep, I am a better person as a whole.

I am making progress with my no/yes list. At first, saying "No" felt uncomfortable. But when I find time for a nap, yoga, a quiet walk, or binge watching Netflix (all of which I have done recently), I feel free. Free of burden, stress, and guilt, I am learning tasks can wait. I can relax. More and more, I am comfortable saying "No," and saying YES to what matters most. I am a better person, better family member, better friend, and, "YES!" a better social worker!

Reflection/Discussion

1. Do you too often say "Yes" when you could and should say "No"? Do you feel guilt or some sort of negative emotion when you say "No"? How might you begin to address these?
2. Is your self-worth based mostly on professional accomplishments or a combination of personal and professional?
3. Think of specific times when you can say "No," in order to say "YES" to yourself.

Selected Resources

Brown, B. (2010). *The gifts of imperfection: Let go of who you think you're supposed to be and embrace who you are.* Center City, MN: Hazelden.

Fink-Samnick, E. (2007). Fostering a sense of professional resilience: Six simple strategies. *The New Social Worker, 14*(3), 24-25.

Morgenstern, J. (2013). Create a saner to-do list. *O-The Oprah Magazine, 14*(2), 114-115.

Richardson, C. (2009). *The art of extreme self-care: Transform your life one month at a time.* New York, NY: Hay House.

Zzzz—Sleep for Self-Care

Carmen M. Rickman

Zzzz...I started to realize something about myself. I was tired all the time. It didn't matter how early I went to bed or how much coffee I drank—I was tired. As I began to think more about what I could do to revitalize the energy I knew I had within me, various ideas started to come together.

It started in a graduate class, where we incorporated self-care assignments. My self-care plan included getting at least six hours of sleep a night—Zzzz time! Sleep is a basic, physical need. From social media, to articles in popular magazines, to research studies, we are increasingly aware of the crucial impact of sleep on concentration, mood, health, and overall well-being. (See *Selected Resources* at the end of this entry.)

But, like many in our busy culture, I have always had difficulty with sleep. Perhaps the following routine sounds familiar to you. After finally falling asleep, I would awaken two to four hours later. Upon awakening in the middle of the night, it would take me at least 30 minutes to fall back to sleep. Constant sleep disruption occurred nightly. It was horrible! Every time I awakened, my brain would start the thought process all over again.

So, as I refined my self-care plan to make it SMART-er, I asked myself: *what can I do?* To make this goal more measurable, I changed my goal to six hours of uninterrupted, restful sleep a night. Then, I created a 3-step Zzzz self-care plan for falling asleep and having more restful sleep.

Zzzz—Step One:
Break a bad habit.

I stopped falling asleep with the television on. (Many sleep experts advise removing televisions and electronic devices from bedrooms. Because of my life context—single mother of a young daughter, living in a relatively small apartment—I have a television in my bedroom for "me" time.) Even though I had my TV set to turn off at a certain time, the background noise still intruded my thoughts. Yet, I had difficulty adjusting, without the background noise. As a result, I tossed and turned relentlessly. My thoughts also continued to keep me awake as my mind needed time to process the day's activities and the next day's agenda.

Zzzz—Step Two:
Practice deep breathing techniques.

I inhaled deeply for five seconds and exhaled for seven seconds. The deep breathing helped me center myself and relax. However, I still had difficulty getting the rest needed to feel revitalized the next day.

Zzzz—Step Three:
Zen Meditation

Through the discussion board conversation with my peers about this challenge, I learned of an abundance of Zen meditation apps for Android and iPhones. I found an excellent Zen app for meditation that included sleep, relaxation, study, exercise, and positive self talk. The *Relaxing Zen Music app* by Think Big Group from Google Play even has a choice of guided or non-guided meditation. It also has different time limits, ranging from five minutes to three hours of Zen sounds.

I found that when I used these three Zzzz steps together, I was able to start sleeping much better.

Although falling asleep with the TV is tempting, because I have gotten comfortable in bed, I make myself turn it off. And if I am still awake when my timer turns off my TV, I leave it off. The timer signals me: It's Zzzz time! I use my phone or tablet to play the Zen sleep music for one hour. While the Zen meditation music plays, I practice deep breathing techniques, allowing my mind the time it needs to process. These three Zzzz techniques have become a normal part of my sleep routine. I awaken more refreshed, revitalized, and prepared for the day ahead of me.

So often, we sacrifice sleep to try to accomplish more throughout the day. We need to remember how much more we can accomplish, in even shorter amounts of time, when our minds are refreshed and our bodies rested. "Zzzz"s for self-care—the perfect way to end the day for tomorrow's new beginnings.

Reflection/Discussion

1. In what way has sleep affected your day-to-day activities, health, and well-being?
2. How are your own self-care strategies for sleep beneficial? Challenging?
3. How might you adapt the three "Zzzz"s strategy to fit your lifestyle?
4. How can sleep be combined with other strategies to make self-care more holistic?

Selected Resources

National Sleep Foundation. (n.d.). Retrieved from *http://sleepfoundation.org/*

Rosenberg, R. (2014). *Sleep soundly every night, feel fantastic every day: A doctor's guide to solving your sleep problems.* New York, NY: Demos Medical Publishing.

Think Big Group. (n.d.). *Relaxing Zen Music app* [Mobile application software]. Retrieved from Google Play.

Chapter 4
Concluding Reflections:
Claiming *Your* ABCs of Self-Care
Erlene Grise-Owens

I am one of twelve children born to parents who, because of their socioeconomic circumstances, did not finish high school. But they emphasized the value of education to their children. One of my childhood memories is the angst I experienced as a pre-schooler when asked, "Do you know your ABCs?" At that developmental phase of literal and egocentric cognition, I focused on the YOUR part of that question. I worried: How will I know *My* ABCs? I suppose, in my budding spirituality, I thought they would have to come by Divine revelation. I surmised that none of my siblings could tell me; after all, they only knew *Their* ABCs.

In retrospect, I joke that perhaps I was just startled to have something that was MINE. In a family of 14, communal property was the norm; from socks to toys, rarely did anything belong solely to one person. Nowadays, as a professor, when students ask me about all the initials attached to my name, I relay this story. I explain that once I learned *my* ABCs, I really wanted to use them! So, I'm obsessed with ABCs!

This *Handbook* covers the ABCs of self-care and offers a range of insights, resources, and reflections. But you are invited and encouraged to learn and claim Your ABCs! Many concepts and practices related to self-care can be universally applied; they are the foundational building blocks. Yet, just as the ABCs can be used to construct myriad sentences and communicate a range of ideas, the possibilities for constructing YOUR self-care plan are exponential. My pre-school logic was well-founded; each of us has our own ABCs. At the same time, we share these common elements.

This *Handbook* project emerged out of a conviction that social workers and others in the helping/human services fields deserve wellness. The co-editors, contributors, and I completed this A-to-Z project as a labor of love. We hope that you receive this product in the spirit of collegiality and shared connection. Self-care is not a finished product; it is an ongoing process! Each of us who contributed to this project will continue to explore and develop our self-care ABCs. We hope this book will be a useful tool, an encouraging resource, and an inspiring gift for many years to come.

Your Invitation: Become *Aware* of your own relationship with self-care. Strive for the *Balance* that works for you. Remember the importance of *Connection* and *Relationships* in self-care. Pay attention to the basics of *Diet, Exercise,* and *Zzzz—Sleep!* Reflect on the effects of *Fear, Gratitude,* and *Humor/Play* on self-care. *Individualize* your plan; take small steps for significant gains, the *Kaizen* way; approach self-care as a *Lifestyle.* Emphasize *Job Satisfaction;* pursue *Organizational Wellness;* use *Supervision* and *Professional Development.* Assess and adjust your *Workspace.* Reflect on your *Values* to sustain you. Practice *Mindfulness;* nurture yourself through *Nature; eXpress* yourself through creativity; and savor *Time.* Develop your *"Yes" (and "No!") lists.* And, always remember: *UR Worth* the *Quality* self-care!

We welcome any additional insights and suggestions, as you learn and use *your* ABCs! Together, let's create a web of wellness in our profession—one self-care plan at a time!

Appendix A

Self-Care Planning Form

If you do what you have always done, you will get what you have always got.

Mark Twain

Care Area*	Specific Goal/ Objectives (SMART)**	Accountability Measure
Physical Care		
Psychological Care		
Social Care		
Professional/ Academic Care		

*Any of these areas can include a spiritual dimension.
**SMART=Specific, Measurable, Achievable, Realistic, and Time Limited.

Appendix B

Self-Care Planning Form—Example

If you do what you have always done, you will get what you have always got.

Mark Twain

Care Area*	Specific Goal/ Objectives (SMART)**	Accountability Measure
Physical Care	• Walk 10,000 steps per day, on average • Get at least 7 hours sleep nightly • Eat a healthy breakfast daily • Do yoga x3 per week	• Fitbit • Log • Sleep App • Calendar • Accountability Partner
Psychological Care	• Read and reflect on spiritual texts and wellness resources 3-4 hours per week • Walk in nature setting weekly • Do deep breathing exercises daily	• Journal • Self-monitoring • Calendar
Social Care	• Talk/text/FB/ Connect with at least four people I love daily. • Eat dinner with family/friends x5 weekly.	• Family & friends • Self-monitoring • Calendar

Profes- sional/ Academic Care	• Attend month- ly book club • Lunch with a colleague at least weekly • Participate in monthly train- ings at work, at least 6 times per year • Block out an hour each day for documenta- tion/office time • Meet with supervisor weekly • Schedule 5 hours weekly at the library to do class as- signments • Phone/meet with study partner weekly	• Calendar • Colleagues • Accountability group • Supervisor • Study partner

*Any of these areas can include a spiritual dimension.
**SMART=Specific, Measurable, Achievable, Realistic, and Time Limited.

About the Editors

Mindy Eaves (CSW, MSW) is the founding Ombudsman for Jefferson County Public Schools, faculty at Spalding University teaching in the Social Work Graduate Program, and a doctoral student at the University of St. Thomas. Mindy is a member of Phi Alpha Honor Society and graduated *summa cum laude* with an MSW from Spalding University. Her areas of interest include critical race theory; prison pipeline; social policy; intersection of race, class, and gender; and social work education. Mindy is a recipient of the Cabinet for Health & Families Award for Excellence, Social Worker of the Year, and Kentucky Court of Justice KLEO Award. Mindy loves quality time with her family and tranquility of nature for self-care.

Erlene Grise-Owens (Ed.D., LCSW, LMFT, MRE) serves as MSW Director and Professor, School of Social Work, Spalding University, Louisville, KY. She has worked in clinical and administrative roles. With almost two decades of experience, she considers social work education her current arena of practice. She has significant contributions in the scholarship of teaching-learning. She is on a mission to positively affect the profession's culture through promoting practitioner wellness/self-care. Favorite self-care strategies include travel, yoga, walking, reading, and practicing rule #6 (i.e., don't take yourself so seriously!).

Justin "Jay" Miller is an Assistant Professor in the College of Social Work at the University of Kentucky. Jay has previously worked as a social worker at the Cabinet for Health and Family Services, Louisville's Crimes Against Children Unit, and the Ireland Army Hospital at Fort Knox. Jay is dedicated to social issues and community outreach, a passion that he brings to his work as an educator and scholar. His research and academic interests focus on child welfare, particularly outcomes related to foster care and adoption. Jay was a Cohort Two Doris Duke Fellow (Doris Duke Foundation and Chapin Hall at the University of Chicago) and earned his Ph.D. at the University of Louisville. Jay enjoys physical fitness for self-care. Last but not least, Jay is a proud foster care alum!

About the Contributors

Donia Addison is a Master of Social Work student at Spalding University. She served nine years in the Army Reserve and completed one tour of duty in Kuwait. She has more than 14 years of experience within the disability community and currently works for a nonprofit agency providing support to parents of children with disabilities. She enjoys local Zumba classes and spending time with her family and friends.

Kimberly Crum (MSW, MFA in writing), is equal parts social worker and writer. After practicing social work in health and mental health care settings, she began to write nonfiction. She now owns Shape & Flow, a writing instruction studio at a repurposed slaughterhouse in Louisville, Kentucky. There, she enjoys leading memoir workshops, attended primarily by persons who want to tell life stories, for posterity or publication. She also critiques academic manuscripts for professors in the social sciences. Kimberly is proud that, for 10 years, she has taught writing seminars to MSW students at Spalding University's School of Social Work. When colleagues and students ask Kimberly why she left social work, she quickly replies, "I didn't leave." Social work and writing require the same skills—careful observation, intuition, a fascination with people and their stories, self-expression and a curious mind.

Tabitha DeLeon has an MSW from Spalding University. She currently serves as a Therapist for Ireland Home Based Services, LLC, in Southern Indiana. She provides therapeutic services to children and families involved with DCS and Probation. She recently served as a Cadet Mentor for Hoosier Youth Challenge Academy (HYCA). She is also trained in Family and Divorce Mediation. When not working or volunteering, Tabitha enjoys spending time with her family, reading, crafting, and watching documentaries.

Wade Drury, MSW, is a graduate of Spalding University in Louisville, KY. He currently serves as a case manager for a behavioral health agency in Hoxie, Arkansas. He works primarily with children who are experiencing severe emotional disturbances. His current interests of study are rural social work, LGBTQ families, and lifespan development. Wade practices self-care by communing with nature, spending time with positive people, and having a good laugh as often as possible.

Tiffany Dulamal has a Master of Social Work from Spalding University. She currently works at The Couch Immediate Mental Health Care alongside psychiatrists, nurse practitioners, nurses, and social workers to provide psychotherapy and medical management to people who need immediate psychiatric care. Her studies and experience are primarily in community health and mental health. In her spare time, she enjoys volunteering, drawing comics, and watching lots of Netflix.

Laura E. Escobar-Ratliff, CSW, MSW, is a Lecturer in the School of Social Work at Spalding University, Clinical Supervisor for Seven Counties Services Rural Division's Assertive Community Treatment (ACT) Team, and is a doctoral student at the University of St. Thomas. Additionally, Laura serves as Treasurer on the board of La Casita Center. Laura's clinical focus has been with co-occurring disorders (mental health and addictions) and teaching focus on practice and policy classes. Laura has committed herself to improving her own self-care skills and teaching others the importance of self-care. Laura's self-care focus is on incorporating self-care into her existing family routine, so the entire family moves toward a healthier balance.

Nicole George is a Certified Social Worker practicing within the field of child welfare. Nicole currently works as a program manager for the University of Louisville working to enhance behavioral health services for Kentucky's children in foster care. Throughout her career, Nicole has worked in various child welfare areas, including frontline practice, supervision, quality improvement, and policy analysis. As a native Louisvillian, Nicole obtained her MSW from Spalding University, where she is involved in alumni activities and serves as an adjunct lecturer. Nicole has an array of civic commitments and volunteer activities. When not engaged in professional and civic work, Nicole is an avid runner and enjoys gardening with her spouse.

Sean McKiernan Hagan, MSW, CSW, CADC, CAP, is an alcoholic, addict, suicide attempt survivor, and adventurer who is clean, sober, and abstinent through 12-Step recovery. He obtained a bachelor's degree in business from the University of Louisville and currently works in the area of addiction treatment. Having had a personality change as a result of his recovery, he decided to devote his life to helping others. He earned a Master of Social Work degree from Spalding University, where he graduated with a 4.0 and had perfect attendance. Sean's essential self-care strategies include 12-Step meetings, prayer, meditation, living by spiritual principles, helping others, world travel, road trips, hiking, camping, bicycling, and walking with his dog, Tiger Lily. His two favorite places to visit are Ireland and the Virgin Islands.

Jillian Harlamert has an MSW from Spalding University. Currently, she works as a Social Service Clinician for Child Protective Services in Louisville, Kentucky. She provides ongoing services to children and families and assists them with overcoming and preventing future abuse and neglect. Jillian's favorite self-care strategies include reading, traveling, and spending time at the lake with friends and family.

Kristin Johnson has an MSW from Spalding University. She currently serves as a Career Planner with Jefferson County Public Schools in Louisville, KY. She works with "at risk youth" empowering high school students to succeed and transition into college and/or the workforce. She provides students with the resources and knowledge to be successful. She assists in addressing students' attendance and behavior issues and works to eliminate barriers for students, parents, and faculty to create a better learning environment. Additionally, she is involved in community activities, including working with the Mayor's Summer Works Program, Louisville's "Be the One" Mentor Challenge, and other community programs and events that benefit youth. When not advocating for youth, Kristin spends her time with family/friends and practices self-care. Favorite self-care activities are Piyo, creating new recipes in the kitchen, and finding new DIY projects.

Ellen Kelley, MSW, LCSW, has a long history working in social services and government. She has worked for agencies as small as two employees and as large as state government and a state university. She presently works in community mental health as a Clinical Trainer at LifeSpring Health Systems in Jeffersonville, Indiana. Ellen's passion is teaching community members Mental Health First-Aid skills. Her own self-care skills include walking, mixed media art, and fixing up old houses.

Eileen H. Krueger has an MSW from Spalding University. As a cancer survivor and mother of three adult children, her interests focus on working with patients and their families in the field of medical social work. She volunteers at the ACS, Gilda's Club Louisville, and is an active member of her favorite charity—Friend For Life Cancer Support Network. Her self-care activities include keeping in touch with her kids, pilates, walking, travel, winter sports, and entertaining.

Kathy Lay has a Ph.D. in social work from the University of Louisville with a Certificate in Women's Studies. She has been a clinical practitioner, working in mental health and substance abuse with individuals, couples, and families for more than 20 years. She is a co-investigator on research projects with an interprofessional team researching SBIRT, tobacco cessation education for mental health professionals, and alternative practices used to facilitate recovery from addictions. Her pedagogy focuses on critical reflection, and she has conducted research on reflection as it relates to clinical practice, service learning, and the classroom. Her research methodology is primarily qualitative with a focus on phenomenology and grounded theory. She is also a Registered Yoga Teacher (RYT 200), has been trained in mindfulness meditation (MBSR) and transcendental meditation, and has special interests in brain-based therapy and teaching.

Tammy Bryson-Quetot is a Licensed Social Worker with an MSW from Spalding University. Tammy works for the U.S. Army Department of Defense as the Survivor Outreach Services Program Coordinator at Ft. Knox. She was responsible for implementing this program seven years ago that provides comprehensive, long-term grief support and services to families of deceased soldiers. Tammy also volunteers for the American Red Cross by facilitating Reconnection Workshops for military members, veterans, and their families nationally. When Tammy is not working, she likes spending time with her family, horseback riding, journaling, and gathering mother nature's love (i.e., heart- shaped rocks).

Amee Ramsey is currently a Master of Social Work student at Spalding University. Life experiences led her to the social work profession, and education is offering the foundation for integration of all parts of herself in the practice of social work. She strives to serve at each level of social work practice with humility and competence. Amee is an advocate for self-care and understands that personal efforts of any size make a difference!

Carmen Rickman is a Certified Social Worker with an MSW from Spalding University. She currently handles multiple roles at various agencies serving as the Development Director at Family Time, Inc. in Jeffersonville, Indiana, and as a Crisis Intervention Advocate at the Center for Women and Families in Louisville, Kentucky. She also volunteers as a Migrant and Refugee Mentor at Catholic Charities of Louisville. When not working or volunteering, Carmen likes to practice self-care by kickboxing, vacationing, and enjoying the company of friends and family.

Andrea Russell has an MSW from Spalding University. She works as a Housing Case Manager at Family Health Centers-Phoenix in Louisville, Kentucky. She assists individuals who are experiencing chronic homelessness adjust to housing. She provides case management in a Permanent Supportive Housing Program using scattered site housing. Andrea also sits on the board at a nonprofit agency that supports women recovering from drug addiction. When not working or volunteering, Andrea enjoys spending time with her family and exercising daily.

Stacey Sougoufara has an MSW from Spalding University. She currently serves as the Social Service Director for Springhurst Health and Rehab in Louisville, Kentucky. She plans, develops, organizes, implements, and evaluates resident service programs of the facility. She develops and implements policies and procedures for the identification of medically related social and emotional needs of the residents. Stacey participates in community planning related to the facility and resident needs. In addition, she maintains quality working relationships with medical professionals and health related organizations. When not working, Stacey attends Boot Camp and juggles her daughter's extra curricular activities—ballet, fencing, and percussion group.

Kaniktra Steadmon, CSW, has an MSW from Spalding University. She is a dedicated SOAR Case Manager at Family Health Centers-Phoenix in Louisville, Kentucky. She assists individuals with disabilities who are homeless with applying for Social Security disability benefits. Kaniktra provides SOAR trainings to other service providers within the community. When Kaniktra is not SOARing, she likes spending time with her family and do-it-yourself home improvement projects.

Derek Stephens has an MSW from Spalding University. He is currently employed at the VA Medical Center in Huntington, West Virginia, where he serves as a mental health social worker while working toward his LCSW. When not working, Derek enjoys spending time with his family, playing guitar, and bass fishing.

Tiffany Thompson has an MSW from Spalding University. She currently serves as the Administrative Assistant for the Spalding School of Liberal Studies. She assists faculty, staff, and students with academic and clerical support. Tiffany also provides reading support as a volunteer tutor for the Every One Reads program. When not working or volunteering, Tiffany enjoys academic research, professional development, and spending time with her family.

Vickie L. Thompson, CSW, received her MSW from Spalding University in 2015. Currently, she is a Social Service Clinician with the Cabinet for Health and Family Services, Department of Community Based Services, in Louisville, Kentucky. She works with abused and /neglected children on the Protection and Permanency Unit. She is a member of the NASW and NASW-KY. In her spare time, she enjoys spending time with family, friends, and working on craft projects.

Geneva White earned her MSW from Spalding University. She currently serves as a Social Services Worker for Child Protection Services in Louisville, Kentucky. She has a strong passion for assisting families that struggle with substance abuse and mental illness. Her self-care activities include spending time with her family and friends, shopping, traveling, and watching movies.

Elena Winburn has a master's degree in psychology (with a concentration in crisis management) and a master's degree in social work. She was born and raised in Russia, and immigrated to the United States in 2007. She has experience in foster care and conducting assessments and trainings with potential foster and adoptive parents. After completing her MSW at Spalding University, she realized her passion for working with military families. Currently, she concentrates on raising her one-year-old daughter. Gardening and crafts are her effective self-care tools.

Ana'Neicia Williams has her MSW from Spalding University. She currently serves as a Program Director at Boys & Girls Club Kentuckiana in Jeffersonville, Indiana. She assists kids ages 6-18 in a positive after-school environment that encourages the development of the whole child by focusing on three priority outcome areas: Academic Success, Good Character and Citizenship, and Healthy Lifestyles. She oversees the delivery of programs in five core areas and plans, develops, and oversees program implementation. When Ana is not working at the Club, she spends time with her daughter and enjoys cooking up new recipes in the kitchen.

Social Work Titles Published by White Hat Communications

Real World Clinical Social Work (published by The New Social Worker Press, imprint of White Hat Communications)
Days in the Lives of Social Workers
More Days in the Lives of Social Workers
Days in the Lives of Gerontological Social Workers
Riding the Mutual Aid Bus and
Other Adventures in Group Work
Beginnings, Middles, & Ends
Is It Ethical?
The Field Placement Survival Guide
The Social Work Graduate School Applicant's Handbook
The New Social Worker Magazine

Visit us online at:

The New Social Worker Online
http://www.socialworker.com

SocialWorkJobBank
http://www.socialworkjobbank.com

White Hat Communications Store
http://shop.whitehatcommunications.com

Network with us:

http://www.facebook.com/newsocialworker
http://www.facebook.com/socialworkjobbank
http://www.facebook.com/whitehatcommunications
http://www.twitter.com/newsocialworker
http://www.instagram.com/newsocialworker
https://www.linkedin.com/company/
the-new-social-worker-magazine